Know Your Heart

Dinesh C. Sharma is an award-winning journalist and author with over thirty years of experience of reporting on issues related to science, technology, health and environment for national and international media. His articles have appeared in *The Times of India, Hindustan Times, Mail Today, Bangkok Post* and *The Lancet.*

His first book, *The Long Revolution: The Birth and Growth of India's IT Industry*, a history of the IT industry in India, was published to critical acclaim in India and abroad. He is a post graduate in Communication and Journalism from Osmania University, Hyderabad.

Dinesh can be reached at dineshcsharma@gmail.com or via the Twitter handle @dineshcsharma.

Know Your Heart

The Hidden Links Between Your Body and the Politics of the State

DINESH C. SHARMA

HarperCollins *Publishers* India

First published in India in 2014 by
HarperCollins *Publishers* India
4th Floor, Tower A, Building No. 10, Phase II,
DLF Cyber City, Gurugram, Haryana -122002
www.harpercollins.co.in

ISBN: 978-93-5136-198-5

2 4 6 8 10 9 7 5 3 1

Typeset in 11.5/14 Adobe Jenson Pro
by Jojy Philip, New Delhi 110 015

Printed and bound at
Manipal Technologies Limited, Manipal

Contents

Foreword vii
Preface ix

Introduction 1
Highway to Heartache 6
Understanding the Risk Factors 23
Of Fattening Burgers and Sweetening Colas 40
Barriers to Physical Activity 76
The Poison Leaf 99
Call to Action 126

Notes 156

Foreword

Don't be fooled by the title. It is not just one more book that glibly tells you how to protect your heart through good living. On the contrary, it is a seriously researched piece of scientific writing that uses sociological analysis to explore and explain why heart diseases are a growing threat to Indians. It does so with a stylistic simplicity that effectively communicates its meaning and message to a reader of any background.

When the millennium development goals (MDGs) were adopted in 2000, heart diseases and other chronic (non-communicable) diseases were not considered important health problems for developing countries and hence didn't find a mention. It was only in 2011 that the United Nations finally recognized these disorders as a major threat to global public health and called for urgent action.

In India too, heart diseases did not feature at all in the national health agenda till recently. This was despite the growing knowledge since the early 1990s that coronary heart disease (heart attack) and stroke (brain haemorrhage) were rising rapidly and claimed many lives in their prime. The effect on families who lost their breadwinners was emotionally and financially devastating while the nation lost more productive person years of life than any other country. Today heart and blood vessel diseases are the leading cause of death in India. They affect all sections of society; even the poor are vulnerable.

To bring about a collective societal response to this threat, it is necessary to educate the government and the people about the causes and consequences of heart disease, combining the knowledge gathered from global and Indian research to develop an action agenda that is contextually relevant. The media can be highly influential in catalyzing such a response. Dinesh Sharma's book will make a signal contribution to this cause.

Through this book, the reader will not only learn why heart diseases should be regarded as a major threat to Indians, but will also become aware of the complex chain of causal factors that stretch from government policies and the industry's marketing strategies to the circumstances that condition an individual's health behaviours. It is the clarity with which this causal web is described that sets the book apart from others that merely prescribe the do's and don'ts about how to avoid heart attacks to the lay reader. Not only are the major risk factors like tobacco, unhealthy diets and physical inactivity described in detail as the behavioural risk factors that lead to biological damage, the political economy of what drives those risk factors in a changing social milieu is incisively dissected. The public health viewpoint prevails over one that is purely technological therapy that seems to fascinate many media persons.

I hope the book will receive the attention of policymakers and civil society opinion makers. It will help bring greater clarity to the policy mix that is needed to prevent cardiovascular disease and catalyze effort on the part of society to protect Indians from the ravages of a largely preventable set of diseases. This book is not just about *your* heart. It is about the nation's heart.

Dr K. Srinath Reddy
President, Public Health Foundation of India
President, World Heart Federation

Preface

More than a decade ago, two seemingly unconnected events occurred in my life. One was a rather routine assignment in my professional career as a science journalist and the other was connected with my extended family. The first one was a workshop to sensitize journalists about cardiovascular diseases in India, which I attended for just two hours. During the workshop, I collected literature that was being circulated. I skimmed through the bunch of papers – reprints of some published studies and a few booklets by the WHO – and discarded most of them. But in the bunch I kept aside to read later, there was a booklet titled 'A Race against Time'. It was about the status of cardiovascular diseases in five developing countries including India. One of its sections mentioned macroeconomic policies and health.

Within a few weeks of this workshop, I received disturbing news from Hyderabad that my elder brother, who had just turned fifty, had suffered a massive heart attack and had to undergo an emergency bypass operation. Many relatives who came visiting wondered, 'Yeh to ameeron ki bimari hain.' They asked, 'How did someone who led a healthy life suffer a heart attack? Isn't fifty too young an age for heart disease?' I was asking myself the same questions and also struggling to find the answers. As I met my convalescing brother, my thoughts went back to the workshop I had attended and to the booklet that had tried to link economic policies and health. I wanted to connect what was unfolding in front of my own eyes, in my own family and in the families of people I knew, with the things experts were talking about. I decided to join the dots. This book is the result of that dot-joining exercise.

Since I started working on *Know Your Heart*, I have seen several people – relatives, friends, colleagues and neighbours – becoming victims of heart disease, stroke, diabetes, cancer and other so-called lifestyle diseases. Both anecdotally and empirically, we have seen a massive wave of heart disease and other lifestyle ailments in India. Now there is far greater acceptance of the problem than there was a decade ago. Yet, the public discourse is largely focused on treatment options, new drugs, healthcare costs, medical apparatus, health insurance and so on. The discussion is also largely centred around the health sector, based on an incorrect notion that it is solely a medical issue. We do not hear much about prevention or the underlying causes behind the rising risk factors.

This book is an attempt to explore the unseen connections between heart disease and policies that impact the risk factors of heart disease. A vast body of literature is available, which is constantly growing, on the medical aspects of heart disease, how to eat right, remain fit and keep your heart young. The focus of all such books is the individual. We need to break this myth. Yes, the individual is important because it is the individual's responsibility to eat right and remain healthy. At the same time, the environment in which the individual functions is equally important. And so are policies that shape this environment. This is the key message of the book.

The book draws data and findings from scientific studies published in peer-reviewed and established medical journals, reports of the World Health Organization (WHO) and other international bodies, reports of the Ministry of Health and the Indian Council of Medical Research (ICMR). Data and information available on websites of various ministries have also been quoted.

In addition, I have interviewed public health experts, cardiologists and researchers in India and abroad. References from popular newspaper articles have also been cited wherever necessary. Some inferences are based on the information gleaned from documents obtained under the RTI Act. All scientific studies and other data used in the book have been appropriately referenced. If there are any omissions, the fault is entirely mine.

I thank Karthika V.K., chief editor and publisher of HarperCollins *Publishers* India, for showing a keen interest in this project and for making valuable suggestions to make the book reader-friendly. Thanks are also due to senior copy editor Bidisha Srivastava and the design team comprising Shuka Jain and Arijit Ganguly for their continued support. I express my gratitude to my wife, Annu Anand, and kids – Maanvi and Kushagr – for putting up with my long absences from family duties while working on this book.

New Delhi, **Dinesh C. Sharma**
May 2014

Introduction

> 'For me the heart has always been an organ without any mystique attached to it ... merely a primitive pump.'
>
> – Christiaan Barnard (1922–2001)

The human heart is like a mechanical pump, a tough machine, which works tirelessly, without a break, right from the time we are born till we die. It has to work optimally for most of the other organs of the human body to function well.

In popular psyche, the heart occupies a special place. It is supposed to depict love, affection, generosity and many other human virtues. Despite modern science and medicine being successful in doing away with much of the mystery surrounding this element of human physiology, the heart continues to fire the imagination of poets, film-makers and advertisers. It is the only part of the human anatomy which figures in literature in almost every language in the world.

The heart, also known as *dil* in common parlance, is a theme of many movies, film songs, television soaps and ad punch lines. More than 150 Hindi films have the word *dil* in the titles – from *Dil Aram* (1926) directed by Nanubhai B. Desai to the Ranveer-Parineeti starrer *Kill Dil* slated for release in 2014. The 1990 romantic drama starring Aamir Khan and Madhuri Dixit was called *Dil*. Thousands of film songs have featured the heart and its exploits as their central theme. A few like *'My heart is beating'* from *Julie* (1975) are all-time superhits.

Every Valentine's Day, the heart generates billions of rupees worth of business through sale of merchandise that feature it in some form or other. The heart also dominates other cultural constructs; even mythology and ancient texts mention it. In Ramayana, monkey-god Hanuman ripped open his chest to reveal Lord Rama etched on his heart.

Scientific advances have helped remove the shroud of mystery surrounding this human organ by deciphering its physiology and functioning. Heart transplants and even artificial hearts are not just confined to science fiction. One of the major functions of this small muscular organ – the size of one's clenched fist – situated slightly to the left under the breast bone, is to pump blood to all parts of the body. On an average, the heart muscle contracts and relaxes 70 to 80 times every minute, pumping about seven litres of blood a minute. The cardiac muscle is sturdy and needs to remain in shape throughout. A network of coronary arteries on its walls supplies blood to the heart. When these arteries get clogged with a glue-like substance called cholesterol, they pose a major health challenge. Hardening of the arteries or atherosclerosis due to the presence of a high amount of bad cholesterol (LDL) is the most common form of heart disease in India. The metaphorical *Dard-e-dil* suddenly seems all too real.

The Risk Factors and their Causes

By all accounts – epidemiological studies, hospital-based data, anecdotal evidence and estimates by national and international agencies – heart disease is on the rise globally. In India, it is already the number one killer.

Unlike diseases caused by viruses and bacteria, which can be treated with antibiotics and vaccines, heart disease is not caused by one but several risk factors. But most of these factors can be modified. It is in our hands to keep our hearts healthy. The World Health Organization has recognized unhealthy diets coupled with inadequate consumption of fruits and vegetables, tobacco use, obesity and physical inactivity as the most common risk factors causing heart and other non-communicable diseases. In September 2011, the United Nations held a special session on heart health and all member countries resolved to initiate steps to address the problem.

If we want to combat heart disease, we need to control our diets (give up unhealthy and energy-dense foods rich in sugar, salt and fats), reduce tobacco consumption, indulge in more physical activity and tackle the obesity problem. The doctor's advice is simple: eat healthy food, cut down on tobacco and alcohol use, remain physically active and lose a few kilos, especially around the waist. The responsibility to do all this rests with you, the individual.

This book explodes the myth that an individual alone is responsible for his or her ailments, particularly heart disease and the underlying conditions like diabetes and hypertension. The book is not about the risk factors but about how they pose a risk. If more and more Indians are consuming unhealthy diets, why are they doing so? If all of us are becoming physically inactive, what's causing the rise in this trend? If tobacco consumption is rising, what's fuelling this spike?

An investigation into these questions reveals something unexpected and shocking: it is the Indian State which is fuelling these risk factors to a great extent. Narrow political interests, faulty state policies and corporate greed are boosting heart disease in the country. How, is what the book talks about.

Take for instance, tobacco consumption. No sane government in the world subsidizes tobacco. The Indian government does. Billions of rupees are doled out in direct and indirect subsidies to this industry. Every rupee that goes as subsidy to the tobacco industry contributes to the clogging of arteries because scientists say that just one cigarette is enough for your arteries to take a hit.

No country that calls itself a welfare state supports the junk food industry. India does. The Government of India tells its citizens that 'processed foods are better than fresh fruits'. Isn't it ironical that billions of taxpayers' money go to companies for the manufacturing and marketing of food stuff that, according to doctors, is bad for your heart?

Only a reversal of these heart-unfriendly policies, coupled with active health promotion measures, can prevent the tsunami of heart disease in India. The developed world has demonstrated that it is possible. Just small policy changes – demotorizing urban spaces while encouraging cycling and walking, boosting public transport, restricting tobacco advertising and marketing, regulating the salt and sugar content in processed foods and food served in restaurants, enforcing labelling, facilitating fruits and vegetable consumption, introducing health promotion policies in workplaces and schools – have sent heart disease cases plummeting in the past three decades. The least India can do is stop subsidizing the risk factors. Is our country ready to learn?

Organization of the Book

The first two chapters throw light on the dimensions of the problem and the emergence of the risk factors. Communicable diseases have gradually been displaced by lifestyle or non-communicable diseases as the top killers. Heart disease has emerged as the number one killer even in the rural areas. The second chapter also deals with the evolution of the concept of risk factors globally and in the Indian context. While certain genetic factors are at play in India, these alone do not explain the rise of heart disease in the past two decades.

The next three chapters deal with three major risk factors: unhealthy diets, physical inactivity and tobacco. India has seen rapid economic growth in the last twenty years, particularly after the country embraced liberalization in 1991. There were major policy changes across all sectors, including agriculture and food, which had a huge impact on the dietary patterns of Indians. The food environment of Indian cities is transforming rapidly. The third chapter discusses this transformation. The fourth deals with the changing physical environment, which is the main contributory factor in the growing incidence of physical inactivity among Indians. The fifth chapter unveils the pro-industry policy framework for tobacco products.

The last chapter provides evidence from different parts of the world of how positive policy changes can help reduce the risk factors and their impact.

Disclaimer

The author hasn't received any direct or indirect financial help, grant or fellowship from any source to write this book. The hypothesis about state policies boosting the risk factors has been proposed on the basis of scientific studies, government data and discussions with experts. All research studies quoted are in the public domain and references have been cited in most cases.

Highway to Heartache

As one drives through any big Indian city like New Delhi, Mumbai or smaller towns such as Ichalkaranji in Maharashtra, Surat in Gujarat or Warangal in Andhra Pradesh, one notices huge billboards on both sides of the road. The shiny flex boards mounted on the steel frames herald the arrival of the latest models of cars and smart phones. Many of the billboards advertise fizzy drinks, pizzas, burgers and a variety of ready-to-eat Indian snacks. Some even have Bollywood stars and cricket icons on them.

A new but surprising addition to the list of outdoor advertisers is multi-city corporate hospitals and pathology laboratories that sell their 24x7 services. These signages are so prominently placed along national and state highways that the traveller cannot help but notice the bait (of discounts) that is offered. The town's 'best state-of-the-art' hospital is not very far away from his current location. The faces on these billboards look so cheerful that its seems as if they are celebrating disease and illness.

Pamphlets of restaurants touting free-home delivery and hospitals dangling discounts on whole body and heart check-up packages vie for the reader's attention in newspapers every morning.

In neighbourhood markets, frequented by urban middle-class Indians, one can spot huge posters and banners announcing

'Free Health Check-Up Camps' organized by hospital chains. And groups of youngsters merrily smoke and chat away on their fancy mobile phones right under these banners. Not far, the not-so-young pop pan masala from shiny sachets while hordes of men and women gorge on hot kathi rolls and samosas. The scene in upscale, swanky malls – the most visible symbols of India's growth story – is no different, though the malls appear much more sanitized and boast hygienic surroundings.

Mini shopping complexes abutting residential areas are hubs of activity, especially in the evenings. One often sees couples arriving in luxury sedans and sports utility vehicles to shop for their daily needs, vegetables and groceries. It is not uncommon to find large cars screeching to a stop right in front of the shops so that the occupant doesn't have to walk one extra step. Even if their homes may be just a few metres away, people prefer to drive all the way.

Celebrating Growth

India's growth story in the post-liberalization era is unparalleled. The average per capita income increased more than five times since 1991 and more than doubled between 1997 and 2005, making it a nation 'very high on consumer aspiration and consumer confidence'.[1] The number of people living below the poverty line has dropped from 36 to 22 per cent between 1993–94 and 2004–05, according to official data.[2] In April 2007, India crossed a gross domestic product (GDP) figure of $1 trillion and the per capita income reached $1000.[3] While it took sixty years after independence to reach a trillion dollar GDP figure, it is predicted that the growth will be faster now and the figure will become $2 trillion by 2015. US-based research firm Dun & Bradstreet projects that India's GDP figure will cross $5 trillion by 2020.[4] The per capita income of states like Bihar and Madhya Pradesh, considered laggards in terms of development, is expected to treble by 2020.

The days of shortages, scarcity and long queues for services are things of the past. For a country where one had to wait for several years to get a telephone connection, the number of mobile phone subscriptions in March 2014 stood at about 896 million. Satellite television has made its presence felt even in the most remotest parts of the country. From just two channels in 1991, the number of television channels is said to be touching 500 now. Of 213 million households, 61 per cent have a television set. The number of Pay TV households is 106 million, which is nearly 5 million more than the US.[5] India is the second largest cable and satellite homes market in the world, surpassed only by China.

Car and two-wheeler sales doubled between 1995–96 and 2003–04. Nearly one million motorcycles are sold every month.[6] The demand for cars is rising by 30 per cent every year. Over 34 per cent of urban Indian households with $10 to $20 daily per capita income have cars.[7] Some small towns like Jalandhar and Aurangabad boast large fleets of high-end cars such as Mercedes Benz and BMW.[8] Sale of luxury products, which commanded a market of $4.76 billion in 2009, is also booming. Based on a huge latent demand for luxury products and services, we may see this market touch the $15 billion mark by 2015.[9]

It is not as if it's only the rich who are spending. The 'great Indian middle class' is growing by leaps and bounds. The size of the middle class has always attracted consumer goods makers and marketers. The population share of the middle class increased from about 29 per cent in 1993–94 to 38 per cent in 2004–05, as seen in the National Sample Survey (NSS), a periodic and nationally representative household survey.[10] This data suggests that in 2004–05, the Indian middle class comprised 418 million people out of a total population of 1.1 billion.

At high growth rates seen in the 2000s, income levels are poised to treble and India is projected to become the fifth largest consumer market, ahead of Germany, by 2025. Nearly 40 per cent of current and future consumption will come from rural areas, and two-thirds of the urban market will be in second-tier towns.[11] In 2011, the

Asian Development Bank (ADB) projected that three billion Asians – one billion of them in India – could become affluent by 2050 if the current level of growth is sustained.[12]

The rural economy is by no means playing second fiddle to the rise of urban India. The per capita income in rural areas has grown at exactly the same rate as in urban India after the liberalization process took off in the mid-1990s.[13] By 2011, about 750 million rural consumers in India would have reached an annual spending level of a staggering $450 billion. With 70 per cent of the population in rural India, it accounts for 56 per cent of income, 64 per cent of expenditure and 33 per cent of savings. There is a remarkable similarity in the choices between the rural rich and the urban middle class. The rural rich are caught in 'an upward spiral of aspirational buying.'[14]

Taboos on alcohol consumption are fast disappearing. Newspapers are unabashedly lobbying for the legal drinking age to be brought down.

A new wave of consumerism and consumption is deeply impacting Indians. Food habits are arguably getting globalized; some would aver, Westernized. Food courts, multi-cuisine restaurants and pubs are pulling the crowds into shopping malls. The number of Indians, as well as the number of times they are eating out, is increasing; the frequency of visits to restaurants for meals increased to six times a month in 2008, compared to 2.7 times a month in 2003.[15] Fast food is becoming fashionable. This change is visible across rural India as well. The penetration of packaged biscuits in rural households rose from 39.1 per cent in 2000 to 64 per cent in 2008. Soft drinks are consumed in 8.4 per cent of rural households.[16] Taboos on alcohol consumption are fast disappearing. Newspapers are unabashedly lobbying for the legal drinking age to be brought down. Young boys and girls are trying out various forms of tobacco, such as the hookah or shisha, without any scruples, something that was unthinkable just a decade ago.

Our newfound prosperity is changing our lifestyles like never before.

The Other Growth Story

It is often hard to accept that along with prosperity and economic boom, which have become a cause for celebration, are discreetly tucked away the risk factors of newer diseases. With our changing lifestyles – the way we eat, commute, work, socialize, spend our free time – the silent epidemic of lifestyle diseases is gaining ground.

Unlike illnesses caused by bacteria and viruses, which are easily identifiable and preventable or treatable with vaccines or drugs, this new epidemic is not a single disease but a group dubbed 'lifestyle diseases'.

One member, friend or relative in almost every family suffers from hypertension, diabetes, heart disease or cancer. With over 65 million diabetics, India has the second largest number of diabetics in the world next only to China, which had 98 million such cases in 2013, according to data from the International Diabetes Federation.[17] The Indian Council of Medical Research (ICMR) put the number at 62.4 million in 2011. The number of Indians with prediabetes conditions was projected at 77.2 million in 2011. The number of Indians with hypertension or high blood pressure is expected to rise from 118 million in 2000 to 214 million in 2025. Diabetes and hypertension are no longer conditions affecting the old, but are striking the young as well.

Heart disease causes three million deaths every year in India, making it India's foremost killer. How is heart disease the biggest killer? Doesn't India have very high infant and maternal mortality rates? And what about people dying of tuberculosis and malaria? It's true that complications during childbirth kill several thousand

> The new epidemic is not a single disease but a group dubbed 'lifestyle diseases'.

women in India every year; and pneumonia, diarrhoea and other infections kill more than two million children. But none of these tops the list. Surprisingly, the leading cause of death in India, including in rural areas, is heart disease, an ailment generally associated with wealthy developed countries. The Global Burden of Diseases (GBD) study, published in *The Lancet* in December 2012, says the ranking of top killers in India completely changed between 1990 and 2010. Diarrhoeal diseases – the number one killer in 1990 – were replaced by heart disease in 2010. Non-communicable diseases have replaced communicable diseases as the factors leading to severe health problems in India.

If India is prospering, as so many indictors show, it should bring with it wellness and perfect health as witnessed in the previous century. Scientific and economic progress have helped us eradicate several communicable or infectious diseases from most parts of the world. Some of these diseases were the chief causes of death in the late nineteenth century and the twentieth century. Plagues killed thousands, influenza and malaria outbreaks killed millions, and so did diseases in the wake of famines. That we could rid humanity of these deadly diseases is a great achievement, though we are yet to completely wipe out some of them from the face of this earth. In fact, we constantly live under the threat of new emerging infections. Yet the same social and economic advancements that helped us do away with deadly infections are paving the way for a new set of diseases. We have seen this in the West, where lifestyle diseases accompanied its march to richness and emerged a big killer.

The leading cause of death in India – including in rural areas – is heart disease. The Global Burden of Diseases (GBD) study, published in *The Lancet* in December 2012, says the ranking of top killers in India completely changed between 1990 and 2010.

It seems, economic prosperity and lifestyle diseases go hand in hand. An analysis of data from 100 countries published in 2005 showed a definite

Economic growth in India has no doubt been dramatic, but it has also led to the formation of an environment in which heart disease, diabetes and hypertension co-exist with malaria and malnutrition.

pattern between national incomes and lifestyle diseases. It found that the 'Body Mass Index (BMI), a measure of obesity, increased rapidly, then reached a plateau, and eventually declined with increasing national income.'[18] Cholesterol, too, had a similar, but more delayed, relationship with national income. However, a blood pressure rise was not so much associated with a rise in income. The possible reasons for an increase in the BMI, according to the study, are systematic changes in diet and physical activity due to increased access to personal transportation, television and manufactured/packaged foods as a result of technological change, urbanization and organization of work. Another similar study based on data from 199 countries, released in early 2013 by the Harvard School of Public Health and a few other institutions, found that the BMI was consistently related to the proportion of the population living in cities, suggesting that urban lifestyles could be one of the major reasons to trigger the obesity problem.

A 2010 report from the ADB states that rapid middle class growth has led to greater obesity and a rise in chronic diseases such as diabetes, cancer and heart ailment – problems earlier considered rich-world issues.[19] It is further accelerated by rapid urbanization so that an ever increasing section of the middle class is exposed to more unhealthy diets, the report points out.

Infosys co-founder Nandan Nilekani, in his bestseller *Imagining India: Ideas for the New Century* said, 'We have to be careful about how our growth is impacting our health as we surge towards higher incomes and rapid urbanization.' He said economic growth in India has no doubt been dramatic, but it has also led to the formation of an environment in which heart disease, diabetes and hypertension co-exist with malaria and malnutrition.

So why should diseases striking the rich make their presence felt in India when Indians are nowhere near the level of affluence enjoyed by rich Western countries? It may take several decades, or even a century, for India's GDP or per capita income to reach the levels enjoyed by North American and European countries. Yet lifestyle diseases are striking us rapidly. This is because, there are significant differences between the kind of growth countries like India and China are witnessing in the twenty-first century as compared to what the West achieved in the previous one.

For a long time, India's GDP grew at a rate of 2 to 3 per cent. It took fifty years for India to double it, to about 7 per cent. It will take only ten years for the GDP to double this time. The average per capita income of India has increased more than five times since 1991 and more than doubled between 1997 and 2005. In the US and Europe, the growth rates were moderate, public health expert Dr K. Srinath Reddy pointed out. This meant that 'the shift from "shortage"-based sickness such as malnutrition to "excess"-based ones such as diabetes, heart disease and obesity occurred slowly with enough time for the policy to catch up.'[20]

India is rapidly transiting from a low-income society to a high-income one. In the US, this transition occurred over a period of nearly a century, whereas in India the process has been limited to just a few decades. The adverse effects of this change, which the US saw over several decades, experts say, would be visible in India over twenty-five years. Clearly, it is not growth per se but the striking pace of growth that is contributing to lifestyle diseases in India. The transition from a complex-carbohydrate, low-fat diet to an energy-dense, high-fat one now occurs at much lower levels of income than it occurred previously, as the ADB report stated.

India is rapidly transiting from a low-income society to a high-income one. In the US, this transition occurred over a period of nearly a century, whereas in India the process has been limited to just a few decades.

When lifestyle diseases emerged as the unintended fallout of economic growth in the Western world in the 1960s, the hypothesis of 'thrifty genes' was proposed to explain the rather sudden shift from 'shortage'-based sicknesses to 'excess'-based ones. The hypothesis, advanced by American geneticist James Neel in 1962, proposed that the human species, during the course of its evolution, was dependent on the procurement of food, a task that involved physical activity.[21] Since food supply was never consistent, ancient hunter-gatherers experienced cycles of feasting and famine, punctuated by periods that necessitated physical activity and rest. Over centuries, these cycles got ingrained in their genetic make-up. Survival during periods of famine was ensured by certain genes that regulated efficient intake and utilization of stored fat. Neel called them thrifty genes. These genes, according to him, continued to allow the body to store fat for times of famine even in modern times, marked by continuous and abundant food availability, resulting in elevated insulin levels and excessive energy stores.

The hypothesis was applied to explain obesity and lifestyle diseases among Pima Indians. Subsequently, thrifty genes were blamed for heart disease among South Asians, particularly Indians, by a few research groups. Some experts argued that Indians carry thrifty genes, which predispose them to diabetes, obesity and heart disease. Some experts are still engaged in actually trying to locate such genes in the human genome. At the same time, it is argued that the hypothesis is not fully applicable to India, because Indians were not deprived till the seventeenth century and famines were sporadic. Famines became more common in the nineteenth century and early twentieth century as the cropping patterns changed. Surely Indians could not have genetically changed in a span of 200 years or so?

> Our genetic make-up has remained unchanged for several millennia and couldn't have changed in just a few decades. The only thing that has changed is our lifestyle, our eating habits, our environment etc.

It is the thrifty genes hypothesis of Neel that has led to the popular notion that Indians suffer from diabetes, obesity and heart disease because they are genetically predisposed to them. The moot point here is: if Indians are genetically destined to suffer from these diseases, why was the problem not this severe half a century or two decades ago? Surely, as scientists point out, our genetic make-up has remained unchanged for several millennia and the transformation couldn't have happened in just a few decades. The only thing that has changed is our lifestyle, our eating habits, our environment etc. Yet the occurrence of heart disease among Indians and other ethnic groups is not uniform. This can be explained by certain genetic factors, which magnify the impact of environmental changes among Indians.

The dominant disease burden is shifting from communicable to non-communicable and chronic diseases. This transition is mainly propelled by social and economic changes.

India of the twenty-first century is going through a reversal of trends from those in the previous one. There is a rapid decline in diseases linked with nutritional deficiency and parasitic infections, and an alarming rise in coronary heart diseases, strokes and cancers. This is the phenomenon that experts call an 'epidemiological transition'. It is usually marked by a change in the dominant disease profile of a society or a country. This, however, does not mean that people in India are not afflicted by infectious diseases any more. Yes, we still have a huge burden of infectious and parasitic diseases. Tuberculosis and malaria remain serious public health challenges. But the dominant disease burden is shifting from communicable to non-communicable and chronic diseases. This transition is mainly propelled by social and economic changes as reflected in rising per capita income, improved nutritional status, better sanitation and healthcare facilities.

Concurrent with the epidemiological shift, India is moving from a state of 'stable population with high fertility and mortality' to a state of 'low fertility and low mortality'. Population experts call it a demographic transition.[22] When this shift is complete, fewer children would be born and fewer elderly people would die. This transition too is gradual and occurs in phases. India is currently at a stage in which the birth rate has dropped but the drop is less steep than that of death rates and, consequently, there is an increase in population. It is slowly transiting to the next stage in which death rates would reach a plateau and the replacement level of fertility would be attained. Yet the population continues to grow because a large number of people belong to the reproductive age group. A third factor, that is, life expectancy at birth, is also at play. In the beginning of the twentieth century, Indian males lived for an average of 22.6 years, while females lived for 23.3 years. By the end of the century, the numbers rose to 62.3 and 65.3 years respectively. By 2021, the average expectation of life at birth for males would be 69.8 years and 72.3 years for women.[23] Heart disease, stroke and cancers are bound to surface as people age.

The Rising Graph of Heart Disease

A report on the burden of disease in India, published by the National Commission on Macroeconomics and Health (NCMH) in September 2005, estimated that the number of coronary heart disease cases in India was 27 million in 2000 – a number that will double to nearly 61 million cases in 2015.[24] The report put average mortality due to coronary heart disease at 4 per cent in the age group of 20–49 years and 6 per cent in those above fifty. All these numbers would go up substantially if other cardiovascular diseases, such as stroke, rheumatic heart disease and congenital heart disease, are also included.

Heart disease has seen a steady rise in both urban and rural India. Its prevalence has increased in urban areas from about 2 per cent in 1960 to 6.5 per cent in 1970, 7 per cent in 1980, 9.7 per cent in 1990 and to 10.5 per cent in 2000. In rural areas, this figure has gone up from 2 per cent in 1970 to 2.5 per cent in 1980 and 4 per cent in 1990 to 4.5 per cent in 2000. These percentages

About 30 million people suffer from coronary artery disease and the annual death rate is about 3 million. These are supposed to be conservative estimates.

actually translate into huge numbers, with a lot of people suffering from coronary heart diseases in both urban and rural areas. Based on epidemiological studies, the NCMH concluded that there were 30 million patients of coronary heart disease in India in 2005. The actual number could go up even more as epidemiological studies exclude many patients with silent and asymptomatic diseases. The prevalence of cardiovascular diseases in rural populations will be lower than in urban populations but will continue to increase. The prevalence among younger adults and women (in the age group of forty years and above) is also likely to increase.

In addition, several other studies on the prevalence of heart disease in different parts of the country paint a grim picture. The estimated adult prevalence (of age thirty and above) of coronary heart disease (CHD) is around 8–10 per cent in urban settings and 3–4 per cent in rural areas. This is a six-fold and two-fold rise respectively between 1960 and 2000.[25] In terms of absolute numbers, about 30 million people suffer from coronary artery disease and the annual death rate is about 3 million. These are supposed to be conservative estimates.

The most authentic proof of the changing, or changed, disease patterns came in 2009 in the form of the first report from a unique ongoing effort called Million Deaths Project executed jointly by the Office of the Registrar General of India (ORGI) and the Centre for Global Health Research (CGHR) at the University of Toronto. The first report of this study was based on an analysis of 140,000 deaths that occurred between 2001 and 2003. The results were shocking – 42 per cent of all deaths were due to non-communicable diseases.[26] Communicable diseases accounted for 38 per cent of all the deaths. The number one cause of death was heart disease (19 per cent), followed by respiratory diseases (9 per cent). In the age group of

25–69 years, heart disease was the cause of 25 per cent deaths. In urban areas, 32.8 per cent deaths occur due to heart disease, while the percentage in rural areas is 22.9. Heart disease was the leading cause of death in all the regions of the country, with the highest proportion in southern India and the lowest in central India. The regional disparity is a result of a variation in different risk factors like diabetes, hypertension, obesity and socio-economic factors. In 2012, the India Heart Watch study was initiated to chart these variations.

Yet another indication of the heart epidemic is actual data from hospitals. Many hospitals in metropolitan cities have observed coronary heart disease emerging as a major problem for over half a century now, though data for early periods is not available. One of the earliest studies conducted by Dr S. Padmavati in Delhi showed that the prevalence of coronary artery disease was 1.04 per cent in 1962. This number went up to 9.7 per cent in 1990, as revealed in subsequent studies. From 1966 to 1970, coronary heart disease was present in 18.4 per cent of all heart disease cases seen at the All India Institute of Medical Sciences (AIIMS). This came down to 16.5 per cent during 1971–75 and to 15.2 per cent during 1976–80, but rose to 19.7 per cent in 1981–85. At Christian Medical College in Vellore, admissions of patients suffering from this disease increased from 4 per cent in 1960 to 33 per cent in 1989.[27]

The Escorts Heart Institute and Research Centre in New Delhi was set up in 1988 as one of the first such centres dedicated to the treatment of heart disease in the country. In the first year, it conducted 118 angiographies, which is an invasive procedure to diagnose coronary artery disease. This number rose to 4092 in 1995, and shot up to over 10,000 in 2005. Similarly, the number of angioplasties – a procedure to clear blocked coronary arteries – conducted at the hospital increased from two in 1988 to 3000 in 2005. The hospital performed eighty-six cardiac surgeries in the first year of its inception, a figure which crawled up to 4280 in 2005. Between 1988 and 2005, over 51,000 heart surgeries were performed, of which more than 33,000 were cardiac artery bypass surgeries.[28] The Apollo Center of

Excellence in Cardiology and Cardio-thoracic Surgery, set up at the same time as the Escorts Hospital, claims to have performed over 100,000 heart surgeries since its inception.

The epidemic is spreading to rural areas as well. A 2006 study in forty-five villages in east and west Godavari districts of Andhra Pradesh revealed that non-communicable, chronic diseases like ischaemic heart disease and stroke accounted for a larger proportion of deaths than communicable diseases.[29] The leading cause of death in these villages was diseases of the circulatory system (32 per cent) with comparable proportions of ischaemic heart disease (14 per cent) and cerebrovascular disease (13 per cent). A quarter of these deaths were in age groups below sixty. The actual number of deaths due to heart disease and stroke could be higher, as nearly one quarter of the unclassified deaths fell into the category of 'sudden death', which researchers believe would likely have been due to cardiovascular causes. Though conditions like diabetes and hypertension do not feature in the overall causes of death in this population, these two conditions would contribute substantially to the high proportion of deaths due to ischaemic heart disease, cerebrovascular disease and renal failure.

The villages where the study was conducted were economically well off and may not represent a typical Indian village, but they serve as a warning that as our rural areas are developing this problem is gaining ground. And it is a major cause for concern, points out Dr Srinath Reddy. Another study conducted in the neighbouring state of Tamil Nadu also documented a large proportion of rural deaths from chronic and non-communicable conditions.[30] Heart disease, stressed Dr Prabhat Jha, director of CGHR, is not an emerging problem any more. He said, 'It has already emerged as a major cause of death in rural areas. We haven't recognized this and don't have adequate programmes to deal with it.

Nearly one quarter of the unclassified deaths fell into the category of 'sudden death', which researchers believe would likely have been due to cardiovascular causes.

For tuberculosis, you have the TB clinics. For malaria, you have the malaria control programme. For cardiovascular diseases in rural areas, we have nothing so far.'[31]

Striking Young

The most worrying fact is that heart disease strikes at a younger age among Indians. On an average, coronary heart disease manifests almost ten years earlier in the Indian subcontinent compared to the rest of the world. In Western countries, cardiovascular diseases are considered a disease striking the elderly and just 23 per cent of deaths due to them occur below the age of seventy. In contrast, 52 per cent of people dying due to cardiovascular disease in India are under seventy.[32] Several other studies have reported the incidence of coronary artery disease in the young to be between 12 to 16 per cent. Others have pointed out that nearly half the deaths due to heart disease and stroke in India occur below the age of fifty years, and about 25 per cent of acute myocardial infarction in India occurs under the age of forty.

According to *INTERHEART*, an international study sponsored by the WHO to discover the links between risk factors and heart disease in forty-six countries, the average age for the first heart attack in the South Asian (Bangladesh, India, Nepal, Pakistan, Sri Lanka) population is fifty-three years, whereas that in Western Europe, China and Hong Kong is sixty-three years. The first heart attack occurs in 4.4 per cent of Asian women and 9.7 per cent of men at ages below forty, which is 2 to 3.5 times higher than in the West European population and is the third highest of all the regions studied worldwide.[33] Several other studies suggested that Asians in general and Indians in particular are at an increased risk of heart attack at a younger age (less than forty), irrespective of whether they have migrated to other countries or are resident Asians. Since the disease is striking the young in their productive years, it is taking its toll on the productive working years.

Anecdotal evidence from practising cardiologists is frightening. Dr Balkrishna Goyal, a doyen of cardiology, said, 'When I started practice [in the 1950s], very few young people used to get heart attacks. It was a disease of the old. Now heart disease is common in the thirties as well, and, in some cases, the twenties. I have seen patients as young as twenty-eight who have suffered heart attacks. It is not rare to see such cases these days.'[34] Dr Prathap C. Reddy, chairman of the Chennai-based Apollo Hospitals Group, says twenty-seven- to thirty-year-olds with heart diseases is a common sight in his chain of hospitals.

Contrary to popular perception, the heart disease epidemic in India has not left women untouched. The general belief is that heart disease is a problem relating to men and that women have some sort of protection against it. For long, pre-menopausal women were thought to be insulated against cardiac problems with estrogen playing a protective role. But this appears to be no more so, at least, for Indian women. Though the prevalence of this disease among women is low compared to men, it is wrong to believe that it does not strike women at all.

Data quoted in the NCMH report shows that the prevalence of heart disease among Indian women is almost the same as in men in different age groups. In the age group of 40–49 years, more women are at a higher risk from heart disease than men in both urban and rural areas. Doctors say more and more Indian women are falling prey to the disease at a much younger age, compared to women in developed countries. They say diabetes, unhealthy levels of good cholesterol, smoking and premature menopause are factors that predispose women to the early onset of heart disease. Many cardiologists report treating women younger than forty-five years of age for heart disease. Women taking oral contraceptives are at an increased risk of development of blood clots.

Doctors say more and more Indian women are falling prey to the disease at a much younger age, compared to women in developed countries.

Conclusions

Information from various sources, such as epidemiologists, hospitals, government agencies and individual observations, points towards one thing: India is in the middle of a heart disease epidemic. The number is rising and it is worrisome. An estimated 30 million Indians suffer from coronary heart disease and three million die of it every year. The nature of this epidemic is different from what was seen in the Western or the developed world. Heart disease in India is no longer an ailment striking the rich or the affluent. It is affecting everyone irrespective of the socio-economic status. People in rural areas are also suffering on account of heart diseases, though the percentages are a notch below that prevalent in cities. Heart disease in India is striking the young, at least ten years earlier than it does in the West. People below forty are being rushed to hospitals with blocked arteries. Yet another typical characteristic of the disease in India is that women are not protected against it, as believed by many individuals and doctors. The number of people affected with the two ailments, which are the key risk factors for heart disease – diabetes and hypertension – is rising by leaps and bounds.

India is not alone in facing this challenge. Globally non-communicable diseases have emerged as the leading cause of death, killing more people each year than all other causes put together. Almost 80 per cent of these deaths occur in low- and middle-income countries. Of the 57 million deaths that occurred globally in 2008, 36 million, that is, almost two-thirds, were due to non-communicable diseases comprising mainly cardiovascular diseases, cancers, diabetes and chronic lung diseases. Cardiovascular diseases accounted for 17 million deaths globally. About one-fourth of all deaths related to non-communicable diseases globally occurs before the age of sixty.[35]

Understanding the Risk Factors

'Over-eating, heavy and fatty meals, worry, sedentary habits and over-indulgence in sleep are the causes of cardiac diseases.'

– *Charaka Samhita*

It may be hard to believe but the factors that lead to heart-related ailments find mention in an ancient text on Indian medicine, *Charaka Samhita,* written in the eighth century BC. The full translation of the Sanskrit sloka from the *Charaka Sutra* about heart disease puts the blame for all causes behind heart disease on *Kapha* – one of the three doshas described in Ayurveda. Charaka prescribed that 'any person desiring to protect oneself from the adverse effects upon his heart, coronary blood vessels and the contents thereof should particularly avoid all that causes mental affliction.'

Charaka Samhita and *Susruta Samhita* mention that symptoms of heart disease manifest due to 'excessive indulgence in incompatible food, suppression of the natural urges, physical and psychological trauma, and fear and anxiety.' Charaka says in the chapter on rheumatic diseases that vitiation of the *Vata* in the alimentary tract, if left untreated, leads to disorders of the heart. The ancient physician describes paleness of the body, fainting, fever, cough, hiccups, dyspepsia, thirst, nausea and anorexia as the general symptoms of heart disease. However, some scholars feel it is difficult to identify well-defined conditions such as congenital or coronary heart disease in Charaka's description of *Hrdroga*, which would seem to include gastro-oesophageal reflux, chest wall abscess and several other pathological conditions. But there are descriptions that could be interpreted to indicate heart disease as understood in modern times.[1] The ideas of ancient Indian medical experts were rudimentary with regard to the structure of the heart, but they possessed considerable knowledge about its functions.[2]

There are forty-six references to treatment of heart disease in the chapters, 'Chikitsa', 'Kalpa' and 'Siddhi'. The text dealing with pharmacology also lists and describes thirteen single drug remedies and 133 multi-component formulations indicated in heart disease.[3]

In the Western world, dissection of human bodies often supported by the Church had become common in the seventeenth century. Autopsy reports published in books provided a glimpse of various diseases and the symptoms recorded for the first time. Bonet's *Sepulchretum*, published in 1679, contained around 3000 case histories of anatomical findings, which mentioned 'ossified vessels, cartilaginous degeneration of the heart muscle and aneurysms'. Many of the findings were suggestive of myocardial infarction. Similar accounts published in the eighteenth century were more detailed and organized. In his paper at the College of Physicians in London on 28 July 1768, William Heberden presented clinical data portraying the disease in its first phase, when clinical symptoms drew his attention before death of the patients due to heart failure.[4] Over the next 100 years, several clinical aspects of heart disease were described by physicians and clinicians, and by the end of the nineteenth century, a great deal of publications in almost every kind of coronary disease existed. Diagnosis of 'angina pectoris' (chest pain when the heart does not get enough blood supply), however, came to the fore only in the beginning of the twentieth century. Medical historians say that the knowledge of coronary artery disease including myocardial infarction became firmly established before 1920, but only a few physicians could diagnose heart patients till the advent of the electrocardiograph.[5]

Risky Business

Despite the growing knowledge of coronary heart disease in the beginning of the twentieth century, it remained an enigma for doctors and epidemiologists. They could only handle diseases whose causes were bacterial parasites or viruses. They were not aware of the methods to map the causes of a disorder that appeared to have a long and silent onset before abruptly announcing itself. The concept of risk factors was a new one.

The first description of risk factors of heart disease was given by scientists in 1967: 'Coronary heart disease affects mainly flabby, sedentary males [or older females] given to excess of cigarette smoking, diets rich in saturated fats, and living with the conveniences of modern, labour-saving devices.'[6] It took several decades for medical scientists to reach this level of understanding about the general causes of heart disease and stroke. This kind of knowledge about the predisposing factors was absent in the beginning of the last century, even though the number of deaths due to these diseases had been on the rise in Western countries. It was only when heart disease and stroke became an American epidemic by the middle of the century that systematic research began.

The United States Public Health Service was anxious to find out the causes of cardiovascular disease, to which it attributed 44 per cent of total deaths in 1948. A young physician, Gilcin Meadors, proposed a project in July 1947 to study a set of healthy people over a long period of time so that factors that predispose some of them to coronary heart disease could be mapped. This was to be done through clinical and laboratory examination and long-term follow-up of such a group.[7] The idea was to see if factors like heredity and behaviours like dietary habits were responsible. The idea finally took shape a year later in the form of a large study by the National

Heart Institute (later renamed National Heart, Lung, and Blood Institute) in Framingham near Massachusetts. The unique effort soon became famous as the Framingham Heart Study (FHS) and turned out to be a landmark, both in epidemiology and in the study of heart disease.

The objective was to figure out the risk factors by following, over a long period of time, a set of people who had no symptoms of heart disease and had not suffered from a heart attack or stroke. Over 5200 men and women between the ages of thirty and sixty-two were enrolled, physically examined and interviewed about their lifestyles. Since then, researchers have continued to return to the town every two years for a detailed medical history, physical examination and laboratory tests. In 1971, a second generation – 5124 of the original participants' adult children and their spouses – was studied. In April 2002, the study entered a new phase with the addition of a third generation of participants – the grandchildren of the original group.

The very concept of several 'determinants' rather than a single one, came to be recognized as a result of this exercise. The first research study published in 1961 about the 'factors of risk' provided evidence that high blood pressure and other predisposing factors 'precede the development of overt coronary heart disease and are associated with increased risk of its development'. This understanding led to the development of various interventions – personal and population-based – targeting these risk factors. An important aspect was that these factors were modifiable. For instance, one could reduce the risk of heart disease substantially by cutting down on tobacco use or introducing dietary changes. The insight was also used to develop effective treatment and preventive strategies in clinical practice all over the world. The reduction in cardiovascular

> The Framingham study helped epidemiologists develop a new concept of chronic disease based more on notions of probability and disease prevention and not on a perfect understanding of the underlying disease mechanisms.

deaths in the developed world has been largely attributed to the identification of risk factors and their modifiable nature.[8]

FHS identified high blood pressure, high blood cholesterol, smoking, obesity, diabetes and physical inactivity as the major predisposing causes for heart disease. In addition, the research yielded important clues about the effects of related factors like blood triglyceride and HDL cholesterol levels, age, gender and psychosocial issues on development of heart disease.[9] The Framingham study helped epidemiologists develop a new concept of chronic disease based more on notions of probability and disease prevention and not on a perfect understanding of the underlying disease mechanisms. Over 1000 research papers have been published from FHS in six decades. The message from Framingham was clear: prevention is possible if the disease's determinants are modified. The first public health step followed soon in the form of the Surgeon General's advisory on smoking and health in 1964.

Cut the Flab

While the Framingham study was an eye-opener for Americans, the problem still hadn't been fully recognized elsewhere, certainly not in South Asia, including India. Early indications about the extent and magnitude of heart disease among Indians didn't come from resident Indians but from Indians living abroad.

Studies done in Singapore were the first ones to report a higher prevalence of heart disease among South Asian migrants compared to the local population. Being a multi-ethnic island, this former colony of the East India Company became a field laboratory for epidemiologists as they could get comparative data pertaining to different ethnicities. In 1959, doctor-couple Dr Thumboo John Danaraj (1914–1996) and Dr Hee-Ong Wong Danaraj reported in the *American Heart Journal* that heart disease was seven times more common in Indians than in other ethnic groups living there. It accounted for 50 per cent of all disease causes in Indian men but it was just 20 per cent in Chinese and, in much smaller numbers, among Europeans and Malays. The mortality due to heart disease was much higher in Indians compared to other ethnic groups.[10] Dr C.S. Muir of the Department of Pathology, University of Malaya, also reported disproportionate early mortality in South Asians among seven racial groups in the *British Heart Journal* in 1960. Both the studies were based on autopsies conducted in Singapore hospitals.

Dr Danaraj speculated that a higher prevalence of heart disease among Indians was probably due to their poor social strata and lack of knowledge to take care of themselves. On the other hand, Dr Muir pointed to differences in the eating habits of ethnic groups. He noted that while the Chinese ate rice cooked in peanut oil and used fish as the staple source of protein, the diet of Indian migrants mainly consisted of 'chuppattis made from atta flour', a large amount of milk and 'cooking done in ghee (clarified butter)'.[11] Clearly, Dr Muir was hinting at a fat-rich diet as being the major causative agent for heart disease among Indians.

Apparently, Dr Muir had submitted his study a few months before Dr Danaraj, but it was published later. So the credit of first publication on the subject was given to Dr Danaraj. The record was set right fifty years later in 2010 by Vivian Rambihar – a Canadian cardiologist of Indian descent – in the journal *Heart* (which was earlier known as the *British Heart Journal*).[12]

In distant North America, Dr Enas A. Enas, a young physician from Kerala, who went to Chicago in 1970, sounded an alarm on the high occurrence of heart disease in Indians living in America based on first-hand experience. He noticed that some of his young colleagues (some in their mid-twenties) in the Chicago Hospital, where he worked, were ending up in the emergency room with severe chest pain. A disturbing

> All those complaining of heart attacks were Indians, they were very young, they led a relatively healthy life, they did not smoke and many of them were physicians themselves.

pattern was emerging; all those complaining of heart attacks were Indians, they were very young, they led a relatively healthy life, they did not smoke and many of them were physicians themselves. Dr Enas was an active member of the American Association of Physicians of Indian Origin (AAPI) and his interactions with fellow doctors further revealed that Indian physicians across the US were suffering from heart disease.

In order to unravel the mystery behind premature heart attacks among healthy Indians living in America, Dr Enas initiated a project called Coronary Artery Disease in Indians (CADI), which revealed a high burden of heart disease among people of Indian origin in America.[13] It showed that the high risk of heart disease among Indians applied just as much to highly educated physicians, including cardiologists, who were knowledgeable about traditional risk factors for heart disease. When the data was compared with the Framingham study, it was found that Indian physicians were four times more likely to develop heart disease than people with white skin. Conventional determinants, that is, smoking, lack of physical exercise, diabetes, high blood pressure, obesity, failed to explain this high burden. Dr Enas observed that the level of lipoprotein(a) was high in the blood of Indians who suffered from heart disease. Lipoprotein(a) is a genetic variant of LDL and it rapidly promotes plaque build-up as well as abnormal blood clotting, both of which lead to a heart attack. People with high levels of lipoprotein(a) usually inherit it from their parents or grandparents and carry a higher risk of heart attack. In many Indians with premature heart disease, Dr Enas says, 'lipoprotein(a) may be the only risk factor they have.'[14]

Singapore once again provided requisite scientific evidence of lipoprotein(a) being a genetic factor in the development of coronary artery disease in 1996. Researchers from the Department of Pediatrics at the National University of Singapore analysed cord blood of 1010 newborns of pure Chinese-, Malay-, and Indian-descent born at the National University Hospital.[15] They found that Indian newborns had the highest levels of lipoprotein(a), while the Chinese had the lowest. This made researchers conclude that Indian children are genetically predisposed to heart disease from birth itself. The difference seen between the babies of Indian origin and other ethnic groups also corroborates what Dr Danaraj and Dr Muir found out four decades ago in the case of adults.

If higher levels of lipoprotein(a) is the main culprit for heart disease, then the incidence of heart disease should be the highest in Africa because people there have high lipoprotein(a) levels. But it is not so. Africa has the lowest incidence of heart disease. Surely something else is acting up, along with faulty genes. Lipoprotein(a) is particularly considered lethal among Indians because of the widespread presence of other factors, such as low HDL, high triglycerides etc. Taken together, six risk factors, that is, diabetes, high triglycerides, low HDL, high LDL, high lipoprotein(a) and high homocysteine, could explain the prematurity and severity of coronary artery disease among both resident and non-resident Indians.[16]

Despite genetic differences, scientists felt that the determinants of heart disease that work in Indians could be similar to those seen in the West. Genes alone couldn't explain the sharp rise of the disease among Indians in the 1990s. After all, the genetic make-up of Indians hasn't changed dramatically in the span of a few decades. Taking up a project similar to Framingham to identify the risk factors among Indians would have meant waiting for several decades for the results to arrive. This couldn't be done as heart disease was already rising in India. The country had a surveillance system for communicable diseases but no such system for non-communicable one.

In the mid-1990s, scientists at St. John's Medical College, Bangalore, began identifying the causes that lead to heart disease among Indians. Much against the popular notion that risk factors among Indians are different since they are genetically different, it was found that the factors among Indians were remarkably similar to those seen in the West. Dr Salim Yusuf, an alumnus of St. John's Medical College, who had gone to Oxford to pursue a D.Phil on a Rhodes scholarship, conceived the idea of large, simple trials, involving a large number of participants from hundreds of hospitals worldwide collaborating on simple research protocols. This, according to him, was a 'conceptual breakthrough.'[17]

What makes LDLs 'bad' cholesterol is a specific protein called apolipoprotein B or apoB, which 'unlocks' the doors to cells and delivers cholesterol to them.

Based on a new approach to clinical research, Dr Yusuf initiated an international study called INTERHEART to determine the links between traditional (smoking, hypertension, elevated cholesterol, diabetes) and emerging (glucose abnormalities, abdominal obesity, homocysteine, nutritional and psychosocial) risk factors for different ethnic and population groups spread across fifty-two countries. For the first time, this study spelt out the predisposing causes of heart disease among South Asians. Nine risk factors emerged from the study, viz., a high apolipoprotein ratio, current and past smoking histories, hypertension, diabetes, a high waist-to-hip ratio, psychological factors (stress and depression), lack of moderate or high-intensity exercise, alcohol consumption and inadequate consumption of fruits and vegetables.[18]

Lipoproteins carry cholesterol and other fats in the bloodstream as little packages and are essential for the normal breakdown of these molecules. Since blood is made up of a substantial amount of water, it is not in a position to transport cholesterol – a lipid that does not mix with water – on its own. In order to move cholesterol in the bloodstream, the body wraps them up in proteins called lipoproteins. These lipoproteins swim through the bloodstream carrying packets of cholesterol to various parts of the body. Two types of lipoproteins play a major role in transporting cholesterol: low-density lipoproteins (LDLs) and high-density lipoproteins (HDLs). What makes LDLs 'bad' cholesterol is a specific protein called apolipoprotein B or apoB, which 'unlocks' the doors to cells and delivers cholesterol to them. On the other hand, HDLs contain apolipoprotein A-1 or apoA-1, which helps clear cholesterol from the arteries, earning it the title of 'good' cholesterol. A high apolipoprotein ratio indicates a higher risk for heart disease.

Besides a high apolipoprotein ratio, other key reasons that emerged for South Asians were smoking, hypertension and diabetes. Alcohol consumption, which is considered protective for the heart among Westerners, does not appear to be so in the case of South Asians because of differences in patterns of drinking. South Asians indulge in binge drinking and consume hard liquor, unlike regular and moderate drinking habits involving wines in Western countries. The rate of consumption of fruits and vegetables were surprisingly lower among healthy participants from South Asia compared to those from other regions despite a lot of Indians being vegetarian.

Another important observation relates to consumption of green leafy vegetables and fruits, which is associated with a lower risk of heart disease. In South Asian households, prolonged cooking of vegetables is a common practice, which may destroy 90 per cent of the folate content. Although physical activity is a positive factor, the proportion of South Asians who regularly exercised was less compared to other regions. The nine risk factors, the study concluded, collectively explain 86 per cent of the risk in South Asians. Thus, modifying behaviour associated with these risks could have a substantial impact. It has been found that people less than sixty years of age are more susceptible to higher levels of risk and this explains why South Asians are prone to heart disease early.

One of the precursors of heart disease is diabetes, known as diabetes mellitus in medical terminology. Having diabetes approximately doubles the risk of a wide range of blood vessel diseases including heart disease and stroke. The ICMR has estimated that diabetes is directly responsible for 9 per cent of acute myocardial infarctions, 4 per cent of strokes and 32 per cent of cataract cases.[19]

Heart attacks can occur in persons with diabetes without pain or other symptoms. It is possible that some diabetics may have fatty plaques in blood vessels but they may not be large enough to obstruct the blood flow. And since the blood flow is still maintained, they may not experience any pain and show other symptoms associated with heart attacks. But the plaque can rupture as fatty plaques in diabetics have thin caps. This sudden rupturing of plaque can completely obstruct the blood flow and cause a heart attack. That is why doctors warn that the first symptom of heart disease in diabetics can be a massive heart attack itself or even sudden death.[20]

For a long time, diabetes was considered a disorder primarily affecting the affluent and the elderly. But in the past few decades this has changed. In September 2011, an ICMR-sponsored study called INDIAB estimated the number of diabetics in India at 62.4 million.[21] Another 77.2 million Indians were categorized as 'prediabetics'. The prevalence in urban Tamil Nadu is 13.7 per cent, while it is 7.8 per cent in rural areas of the state. In Jharkhand, the figure was 13.5 per cent in urban and 3 per cent in rural areas. Chandigarh, which is the joint capital of two prosperous states – Punjab and Haryana – with 14.2 per cent prevalence, has very high level of diabetes.

The International Diabetes Federation (IDF) cites three main reasons for the spiralling cases of diabetes in India: economic growth (which is leading to a decrease in physical activity and consumption of unhealthy diets that are the major factors causing diabetes), life expectancy (the proportion of the population over fifty years is expected to increase from 16 to 23 per cent between 2010 and 2030) and urbanization (the proportion living in urban settings will increase from 33 to 46 per cent). It has warned that economic growth in India will lead to a greater rise in diabetes than projected, because more affluent rural areas are already reporting a higher prevalence

> Having diabetes approximately doubles the risk of a wide range of blood vessel diseases including heart disease and stroke.

than less affluent ones, thus establishing a link between economic growth and diabetes.

After studying several factors in the population – body mass index, waist size, blood pressure, education levels, smoking, physical activity and abdominal fat – an ICMR-WHO study zeroed in on three most important determinants of heart disease among diabetic Indians: abdominal obesity, physical inactivity and urban living. 'Abdominal obesity' in this study was defined as a condition where the waist circumference was 90 cm or more in men and 80 cm or more in women. Physical activity was categorized as sedentary, moderate or vigorous based on factors such as activity at work, long-distance travel and recreational activity. The rate of abdominal obesity was the highest in south India (39.6 per cent), followed by north India (34.2 per cent), east India (20.7 per cent) and west India (19.7 per cent). This explains why even lean Indians have diabetes. Abdominal obesity is the culprit.

Abdominal fat is emerging as a real cause for concern. Dr Viswanathan Mohan, diabetologist and lead author of the ICMR-WHO study, said, 'We found that in people without abdominal or central obesity and in those who are physically active, the prevalence of diabetes is only 1.8 per cent even in urban areas. This goes up almost ten-fold when abdominal obesity and physical inactivity are present.'[22]

Genetic factors that determine distribution of fat in the body and glucose metabolism in Indians are not yet fully understood. A few Indian studies have shown that while some genes appear to increase the susceptibility of Indians to diabetes, some so-called protective genes found in Europeans do not seem to play the same role in Indians.[23] Indian researchers are engaged in unravelling these genetic factors. However, it is not the genes alone that are responsible for the diabetes epidemic in India. Dr Mohan emphasizes that 'It is highly unlikely that the frequency of genetic variation has changed significantly in this population during the last thirty years.'[24]

> The Jaipur Heart Watch has identified obesity, in particular belly fat, as being a powerful factor behind high blood pressure or hypertension.

High blood pressure (BP) is another factor directly associated with the risk of heart disease. High blood pressure, also called hypertension, refers to high pressure or tension in the arteries that carry blood from the pumping heart to all the tissues and organs of the body. Blood pressure is denoted by a set of two numbers. The one on top – the systolic blood pressure – corresponds to the pressure in the arteries as the heart contracts and pumps blood into the arteries. The one in the bottom – the diastolic pressure – represents the pressure in the arteries as the heart relaxes after each contraction. The diastolic pressure reflects the lowest pressure to which the arteries are exposed. High blood pressure is dangerous because it makes the heart work too hard and contributes to atherosclerosis or hardening of the arteries.

It is estimated that high blood pressure or hypertension is directly responsible for 57 per cent of all stroke deaths and 24 per cent of all coronary heart disease deaths in India. Hypertension is a controllable disorder and a mere 2 mm Hg population-wide decrease in blood pressure can prevent 151,000 stroke and 153,000 coronary heart disease deaths every year.[25]

Though the basic causes of essential hypertension are not known, there is a general consensus within the medical community that excessive salt intake is an important factor, in addition to obesity, tobacco use, advancement in age and genetic factors. A large population-based study called the Jaipur Heart Watch has identified obesity, in particular truncal obesity, as being a powerful factor behind hypertension.[26] Other risk factors are smoking, alcohol intake, physical inactivity, excess intake of dietary sodium and fat, low intake of potassium and fibre, and psychosocial stress.

A direct relationship between the average sodium intake of a population and increase in the degree of blood pressure with aging was observed in a large study called Intersalt, spanning thirty-two countries including India. Sodium helps to maintain the concentration of body fluids at their correct levels. It also plays a central role in the transmission of electrical impulses in the nerves, and helps cells to take up nutrients. When the level of sodium in our body goes up, the body retains too much water and the volume of the body fluids increases. This, scientists believe, could cause high blood pressure, which in turn is linked to a greater risk of coronary heart disease and stroke.

Salt is an integral part of the eating habits of Indians. Dietary habits of Indians indicate that the salt intake in India is quite high. Several Indian studies have pointed to the link between a higher salt intake and the presence of high blood pressure in different population groups. Besides the use of salt in all traditional meal preparations, Indians also consume pickles, chutney, papad, a variety of digestive tablets and powders and salty snacks that have a lot of salt. People in some parts of the country consume salt in excess because of typical dietary habits. For instance, Kashmiris drink boiled tea in which they add salt. A study conducted in the farming communities in three villages in northern Kashmir found that the mean daily salt intake of regular drinkers of salty tea was 10.1 grams, and the daily salt intake was significantly higher in those with elevated blood pressure.[27] Salt consumption was found to be a significant predictor of hypertension even in a rural community in a study done in villages around Varanasi.

The Chennai Urban Rural Epidemiology Study (CURES) found that the mean dietary salt intake was 8.5 grams per day among urban people residing in Chennai, and this figure was much higher than 5 grams per day recommended by the WHO.[28] The study noted that a higher salt intake was associated with older age and a higher socio-economic status, possibly due to an increased intake of 'westernized foods' that were high in salt content. People reporting a high salt intake had a significantly higher prevalence of hypertension than those consuming lesser quantities of salt. The link between salt intake and hypertension was much stronger even after taking into account the effect of other risk factors.

Conclusions

The general idea

Some think heart disease is not such a big problem as is being made out by hospitals, drug companies and the media. Others consider it to be similar to what prevails in other parts of the world. Many of those who are aware of the problem believe in the theory of genetic predisposition. This gives rise to complacence and a notion that if we are genetically programmed to catch this disease, why bother too much about diet and exercise. Some feel that since Indians are predominantly vegetarian and do not use labour-saving devices, they are fit and will be protected from heart disease. The generally skinny body structure – compared to the stereotypical images of bulky Westerners – makes Indians feel that obesity (and heart disease) is not their problem.

The reality

Indians are somewhat unique when it comes to coronary heart disease. A number of studies in the past half a century – since the time of Dr Danaraj and Dr Muir – have provided ample proof of this. The vast difference in the occurrence of heart disease among Indians and other ethnic groups seen by Dr Danaraj in the 1950s is present even now. In fact, new research points to something even more disturbing. The general wave of development and urbanization, along with adverse changes in lifestyle – greater rates of obesity, physical inactivity, smoking and intake of saturated fats – have gone up for residents of Singapore. But the increase in the risk factor levels has had a greater adverse effect on Indian-Singaporeans than on Chinese-Singaporeans. It has led to proportionately more heart disease among the Indians than the Chinese as measured in the incidents of heart attacks and deaths from heart disease.[29] Though the incidence of disease among the Chinese has gone up due to the adverse risk factors, the level of difference between Indians and Chinese seen five decades ago remains the same. Thus an increase in the number of risk factors has had an amplified effect among Indians.

'It is difficult to say what the reason behind this susceptibility is, whether there is a genetic basis, though nothing has been proven yet, or whether there are programming factors responsible from pregnancy onwards because of low birth weight. But the fact of the matter is, whenever we are exposed to an environmental challenge, we seem to manifest the risk much more than anybody else,' Dr K.S. Reddy says.[30] The simple solution, in his view, is to minimize environmental exposure. While it may be useful to conduct research on the gene-environment interaction and find out the programming factors, it may not be an answer to the problem because we may not be able to fix the genes of one billion people.

It is a multitude of determinants – some traditional and some new – which are responsible for the growing threat of heart disease in India. Almost all traditional risk factors, such as unhealthy diets, smoking, obesity, hypertension and diabetes, which have been observed to cause cardiovascular disease in the West are at play in India. At the same time, there is some variation. The overall obesity among Indians may not be as high as that in people from some developed countries, but we have a higher prevalence of abdominal obesity that plays a key role in development of diabetes. This type of obesity can lead to heart disease. For any given body weight, the proportional amount of body fat in Indians is higher. Dr Sonia Anand, professor of medicine at the McMaster University, reported in 2011 that South Asians have 'a lower capacity to store fat in subcutaneous adipocytes than white Caucasians' and therefore 'excess fat overflows to ectopic compartments in the abdomen and liver'.[31] She actually measured fat under the skin and around organs in the abdomen through biochemical tests, MRIs and by taking fat samples with the help of needles in a group of South Asians and white people living in Canada.

> Most of the traditional predisposing factors like unhealthy food, tobacco use and physical inactivity can be modified and heart disease risk minimized.

The study observed that young healthy South Asians have significantly lower levels of adiponectin (a protein hormone secreted by fat cells which regulates the metabolism of lipids and glucose) compared to their white Caucasian counterparts. Low levels of adiponectin are associated with reduced insulin sensitivity. On the other hand, white Caucasians appear to be relatively protected from reduced adiponectin until they reach very high BMIs. This means that even if there were small changes in body weight, it would have a negative impact on Indians.

Tobacco consumption patterns among Indians also vary. Along with high smoking rates, Indians are also inclined towards chewable tobacco. In terms of diet too, a large majority of Indians are not meat eaters, but the fat, salt and sugar content in any traditional vegetarian Indian dish is quite high. In addition, consumption of junk food high in salt and fat content is on the rise. At the same time, they do not consume a lot of vegetables and fruits. Physical activity levels are also dropping and this contributes to the problem. While moderate alcohol consumption is seen as protection for the heart in the West, its protective effect on Indians is not only absent; it has harmful effects as well. Genetic factors are also at work.

The only silver lining is that most of the traditional risk factors like unhealthy food, tobacco use and physical inactivity can be modified and the risk of heart disease minimized.

But are we doing anything to minimize the risk? Or are we encouraging these risk factors? The next three chapters will examine this.

Of Fattening Burgers and Sweetening Colas

> 'Processed foods are as healthy as fresh fruits.'
>
> – Ministry of Food Processing Industries, Government of India*

> 'Adequate consumption of fruit and vegetables reduces the risk of cardiovascular diseases ... High salt consumption, saturated fats and trans-fatty acids are linked to heart disease.'
>
> – World Health Organization**

If you wish to unravel the mystery behind the spate of heart attacks in India, you don't need to go to your doctor or seek expert opinion from an epidemiologist. Begin your journey from your kitchen and neighbourhood market. Take a sneak peek into the shelves of your modular kitchen and jumbo-sized refrigerator. If an inventory of all the items is made, the list would read something like this: rice, wheat flour, lentils, spices, breads, biscuits, cookies, potato chips, noodles, pasta, refined oil, ghee, tea, coffee, idli and dosa mixes, pickles, jams, sauces, tamarind paste,

* From the IEC (Information, education, communication) campaign of the Ministry of Food Processing Industries in print media in April 2011

** 'Global Health Observatory: Unhealthy Diets,' WHO, website: www.who.int

garlic paste and a whole lot of ready-to-eat mixes. The fridge will have chocolate bars, sweets, butter, aerated drinks, canned milk, margarita, cheese slices and spread, paneer, assorted dips, and, in case you are non-vegetarian, eggs, meat and fish as well. Did you notice something? Almost everything on your kitchen shelves and the fridge is packed, processed – some of them ultra processed – and everything is branded.

Now imagine your kitchen in the early 1980s. You would have noticed only a few packed or branded food items. Besides rice and wheat (and flour grounded in a *chakki* or neighbourhood mill), you would have seen other grains like jowar, bajra, ragi (depending on which part of India you lived) as well as jaggery (gur), oils extracted from various seeds in a *ghani* and perhaps home-made ghee; and, practically, no bakery items except some biscuits. If you go further back in time to the 1970s, you wouldn't find any packed items at all and perhaps the kitchen would have had no fridge. Even common spices such as chilli, turmeric, coriander seeds and garam masala would have been grounded by hand-operated stone mills. Appliances such as a *chakki* (a hand-operated flour machine) and a *haman dista* (mortar and pestle) used to be an essential part of an Indian kitchen. If you are very young, your mother or grandmother can give you an idea of what a kitchen looked like thirty or forty years ago.

You would notice a similar change on the shelves of a grocery store in your neighbourhood market (mall or superstore). The practice of dispensing loose grains, spices, lentils and sugar has almost completely disappeared. Nearly every item sold in the ubiquitous kirana stores is processed, packed, tinned and factory-made. Such stores themselves are under threat from organized retail in food and other consumer goods. Products being sold in stores may have come from different parts of India and perhaps from several countries around the globe.

In effect, the food environment in which we live today has drastically changed in the past thirty or forty years. Just as the natural environment in which we live – the air we breathe, the water we drink, the soil in which we grow food and plants – there is a food environment. The food ecology is made up of a home-food environment (food available inside the house), a food-store environment (food available in grocery stores, supermarkets, convenience stores, farmers' markets etc.), a public facility food environment (cafeterias, street food shops, vending machines, snack shops, food stalls at airports, hospitals and other public places) and a restaurant-food environment (fast food and full-service restaurants). In addition, we have a school-food environment and worksite-food environment (canteens, cafeterias, vending machines and snack shops in private offices, government buildings and factories).

The process of change continues and some of it has been positive. Consumers have a wider variety of food products to choose from. Hygiene standards have improved a great deal. Packaging helps store products for a long period of time. The home-food environment, which is affected by changes in the macro food environment, has been transformed completely as illustrated above. These changes are critical since what we eat and how we eat is determined, to a great extent, by the food environment in which we live, work, study and travel. Of course, food habits are also influenced by individual factors such as income, ethnicity, religion (preference for vegetarian food or abstinence from meat on certain days) or social environment or networks (family, friends, peer group).

Field studies have shown that food environments impact food habits and health. For instance, the availability of fast food in the neighbourhood is directly linked to an individual's fast-food consumption. A study conducted in Birmingham, Chicago, Minneapolis and Oakland found that the relationship is particularly noticeable among men who had access to fast food between one and three kilometres from their homes.[1] Nearly three-quarters of Californian teenagers live or go to schools in neighbourhoods that are full of fast-food restaurants and other outlets that sell unhealthy food compared to those that sell healthy food. Teens who live or go to school in such neighbourhoods are more likely to drink soda and consume fast food. It means you are likely to eat more junk food if you live in a place where there's a fast-food restaurant or convenience store in every street corner.[2]

The connection between diet and health, in general, and heart disease risk factors, in particular, has been long established by epidemiologists and nutrition scientists. If lack of proper nutrition causes malnourishment and its associated disease conditions, over-nutrition and consumption of an improper diet are the major factors causing heart disease and other lifestyle disorders. American physiologist Ancel Benjamin Keys was the first to demonstrate a connection between cholesterol and heart disease.[3] He discovered that in places such as America, where fat was a major component of every meal, or Finland, where butter or cheese was often spread on bread, the level of cholesterol in blood was the highest and deaths due to heart attacks were rising. On the other hand, in places where diet consisted of fresh fruit and vegetables, bread and pasta, and plenty of olive oil – like in and around the Mediterranean – the blood cholesterol level was low and heart attacks were rare. This led to further research that showed that diet is one risk factor that can be modified or changed to yield positive results for one's health.

The changes in the food environment have resulted in increased supplies of beverages with a high sugar content and processed food high in salt, fat and sugar, which, according to the WHO, are the leading predisposing causes for chronic non-communicable diseases along with alcohol and tobacco. The most visible manifestation of this is rising obesity. Mexico, where the per capita consumption of soft drinks is 300 litres per year, has the highest rate of obesity among developing countries. A Canadian study found that the 'availability

The connection between diet and health, in general, and heart disease risk factors, in particular, has been long established by epidemiologists and nutrition scientists.

of fast food and scarcity of outlets for natural ingredients within 800 metres of a person's home is associated with weight gain.'[4] This, according to researchers, may help explain the observed connection between the geographic concentration of fast-food restaurants and hospital admissions for acute heart attacks.

Mapping India's Food Ecology

The macro food environment depends on multiple factors like food and agriculture policies, land use and transportation policies, and political and economic environments. The shape, size and influence of the food and beverage industry play a major role in defining the macro food environment. Linked to this is food marketing and expansion of media, food production and distribution systems. Understanding these factors that shape India's food ecology is critical to solve the jigsaw puzzle of heart disease.

Policies governing food production, pricing mechanisms, subsidies, taxation, public distribution and school food guidelines play a pivotal role in shaping food environments. However, food environments can often evolve in the absence of specific policies or those which may not be promoting health.[5] In India, policies have influenced food environment in ways that are resulting in transformative changes. But these policies are not health friendly. Some components of the food environment have changed in the absence of policies. In some other cases, it is the food industry which is driving the policy agenda.

The changing pattern of food consumption in India is part of a broader trend observed across the developing world with economic growth. The change is occurring both in terms of the range of food items consumed as well as in the form of a shift away from traditional foods. Barry Popkin, who

Some components of the food environment have changed in the absence of policies. In some other cases, it is the food industry which is driving the policy agenda.

first coined the term 'Nutrition Transition' to explain the shift in diets coupled with physical activity, has over the years tracked the changes occurring in several developing countries across the globe. These studies, in conjunction with the data collected by the UN Food and Agriculture Organization, point to three clear trends: a very rapid increase in vegetable oil intake across Africa, the Middle East and Asia; rising consumption of high-fat-based diets (that were once found only in very rich countries) in lower-income countries; and a major growth in added sugar intake across lower and middle-income countries.

Dietary change is a slow process occurring in stages. As a country progresses economically and the incomes of its citizens increases, diets diversify, yet their traditional features predominantly remain intact. People are able to afford a balanced and more varied diet with the inclusion of nutritious food products. They may still continue to consume traditional staples like rice and wheat but the quality of this food changes. This kind of change in diets helps improve the nutritional status of the poor. Such income-induced diversification was noticed in India in the 1980s and has continued till date.

As incomes spiral up further, profound changes take place in diets. They start getting globalized as people adopt markedly different diets that no longer conform to traditional eating habits. They begin to express strong preferences for highly processed convenience foods and drinks available in supermarkets and fast-food outlets, fruits and vegetables procured from different regions and countries as well as processed meat or fish. In effect, globalization alters 'the quantity, type, cost and desirability of foods available for consumption' by affecting changes in production, procurement and distribution of food.[6] A necessary implication of globalization, according to experts, is 'severing of the link between diets and the local availability of resources and local habits'. Consumers have access to a variety of food not previously available to them. Both diet diversification and globalization are dynamic processes and are moderated by the ongoing changes in policies as well as food environments. Given the size of India and varying income levels of its people, both diet diversification and diet globalization are said to be occurring among different sets of people at the same time.

While diversification of diets is good for improvement of the nutritional status of people, diet globalization, which is being witnessed among the middle class and affluent sections of the society, has adverse health implications. It is far more serious than mere diversification because experts say once traditional food consumption habits are displaced by new consumption patterns, the change becomes largely irreversible as seen in the West.[7]

Dietary changes occur at the family level, but over a longer period these changes begin to reflect in the overall food consumption patterns. Data collected by various government agencies like the National Nutrition Monitoring Bureau (NNMB) and the National Sample Survey Organisation (NSSO) is indicative of the changing dietary patterns.[8] A drop in consumption of cereals in both urban and rural areas has been seen since 1971, despite the falling costs of cereals and their increased availability. The per capita monthly consumption of cereals has come down from 14.9 kg in 1983 to 12.2 kg in 2004–05 in rural areas, while urban areas have witnessed a decline from 11.6 kg to 9.9 kg during the same period. Consumption of pulses – a major source of protein in Indian diets – has also registered a fall.

The NSSO data shows that the 'food energy' consumed by families in the higher-income strata in urban areas is derived from larger quantities of sugar, oil, milk and milk products and smaller quantities of cereals. In addition, intake of 'fat calories' has doubled since the mid-1980s. Meat consumption is growing, and so is consumption of milk and eggs. In rural areas, however, the per capita consumption of fats, oils, sugar and jaggery has not seen a significant rise. Per capita consumption of edible oil has also risen – 30 per cent in rural India and about 18 per cent in urban India between 1993–94 and 2004–05.[9]

People in high-income groups consume more energy-dense food items and engage in less energy-spending activities than people in lower-income groups, as per the NNMB data. This unhealthy combination of high-energy consumption and low-energy expenditure explains the increase in overweight and obesity observed in affluent segments of the population.[10] However, when the per capita income witnessed a sharp increase in the 2000s, there was a relative decline in the energy intake. The decline in energy intake, says nutrition expert Prema Ramachandran, is mainly due to the changes in lifestyle and consequent reduction in energy requirement. This view is supported by the fact that while expenditure on food is declining as a proportion of the household expenditure, the expenditure on transport (an indicator of reduced physical activity) has shown a continuous increase over this period.[11] The energy requirement is sliding in rural areas as well with the spread of piped drinking water supply, better roads and transport facilities. All this means that the calorie requirements of people have gone down to some extent due to decreased levels of physical activity and, therefore, they need to specifically indulge in some kind of physical activity.

A change in lifestyle – resulting in greater access to a diversified basket of food, use of labour-saving devices, automated mode of transport – is inevitable with rising income. All such signs of development and prosperity are welcome. Such changes may be aspirational too. The intent behind discussing these changes is to understand the causes behind the rising tide of lifestyle diseases, and not to argue for a return to the old days of scarcity and under-nutrition or to undermine aspirations. A call to become health conscious should not be seen as anti-development or anti-progress. Prosperity and health should be able to coexist.

India's Brown Revolution

It is critical to understand how and why the food environment of our cities and towns is changing so rapidly. Food and diet are

All policies governing agriculture production, food processing, supply chain, public distribution, food marketing, food processing and food standards play a role in food choices, both at the point of purchase and in individual dietary preferences.

culture-specific issues and depend on an individual's choice, yet the decisions relating to them are influenced by government policies such as taxation, subsidies and import and export. This makes the context of a host of food-related policies significant from the health perspective. Dietary changes should be examined in the backdrop of policies related to the entire food chain – from the farm to the dining table. All policies governing agriculture production, food processing, supply chain, public distribution, food marketing, food processing and food standards play a role in food choices, both at the point of purchase and in individual dietary preferences.

Diversification of diets is mainly a result of the rise in incomes while their globalization is multi-factorial. The demand for packaged, processed, ultra processed, pre-cooked and Western-style food items is growing with the rise in income as well as the process of urbanization. Nuclear families living in cities tend to have double incomes but the woman or man of the household has little time for traditional cooking. In addition, the growing number of working women and single persons living away from home for work or for studies are contributing to this trend. Some observers feel that even housewives have the mindset of working women. On the supply side, a series of policy changes brought into effect in the 1990s have determined the availability of food items in the market.

The integration of the Indian economy with the global economy – a process that began in 1991 – was a turning point in the history of modern India. Tariff walls were demolished and doors were opened for foreign investment in different sectors. Liberalization meant opening up of the food sector to multinational corporations through the Foreign Direct Investment (FDI) route, reduction in freight and transportation costs, import of technology and machinery for food processing, as well as storage and the state-sponsored promotion of the food processing industry.

Active government involvement to promote processed food started several years before economic liberalization began on a large scale in 1991. The first signals of the government's willingness to allow Indian and foreign corporations to play a big role in Indian agriculture came shortly after Rajiv Gandhi became the prime minister following the general elections in 1984.

Just seven years after Coca-Cola exited India over the dispute on dilution of equity structure in 1977, its arch rival PepsiCo made a bid to enter the Indian market. In order to deflect a likely opposition to its entry, the cola giant proposed that it would form a joint venture company with an Indian partner (keeping its equity below 40 per cent in conformation with the foreign exchange rules), which would not only manufacture its soft drinks but would also earn foreign exchange through export of agricultural products. Policymakers were told that this would bring in 'new food processing and packaging technologies to India'.[12] These arguments found patient listeners in the top echelons of the government, particularly the prime minister's office, which had a new set of advisors including Dr Ashok Ganguly, who was the then chairman of Hindustan Lever Limited, a Unilever subsidiary in India. The PepsiCo president is reported to have met Rajiv Gandhi when he visited the US in June 1985 and presented his proposal.[13]

After some hectic lobbying, PepsiCo filed an investment proposal, along with a government company called Punjab Agro Industries Corporation and Voltas Limited, a company owned by the Tatas, for setting up a joint venture for processing fruits, vegetables and food grains in Punjab coupled with its soft drink business. This became a test case for the entry of multinationals in the Indian farm sector. The proposal went through as many as fourteen inter-ministerial panels. Critics questioned if the proposal would 'ruin Indian health by getting people hooked on to potato chips and other junk food that the Pepsi venture would produce.'[14] The Ministry of Food and Civil Supplies opined that 'India should promote fruit juices, not carbonated soft drinks.'[15]

Pepsi got a green signal in September 1988. The deal included setting up an agricultural research centre attached to the Panjab University with a focus on 'processing potatoes for sale here and abroad as fried chips and other fast foods'. It marked a major shift in policy, as noted by a political commentator then, in which 'an important role is to be assigned to multinationals in the farm sector'.[16] It was dubbed the beginning of the 'Brown Revolution' in Punjab, which had been the cradle of 'Green Revolution' two decades ago.

The 'Brown Revolution' has continued to sweep India since 1988. Ironically, a food product that is categorized as the topmost junk food by health experts is in fact the biggest success story of the Ministry of Food Processing Industries (MFPI). The central government must be given the dubious 'credit' for stimulating the consumption of aerated or soft drinks in India and making it a consumer item that has penetrated even rural areas. It is surprising that though sugary aerated drinks are not actually 'processed food' by any stretch of imagination, multinationals making it have become the poster boys of the MFPI. Soft drinks form the third largest segment of the packaged food industry – after packed tea and packed biscuits. The Indian aerated soft drinks industry has over 100 plants, with Coke and Pepsi claiming a combined market share of around 95 per cent.

The cola industry has been growing at a rate of 6 or 7 per cent annually and the government sees a great potential for the growth of this industry since the 'penetration levels of aerated soft drinks in India are quite low compared to other developing and developed markets.' The per capita consumption of soft drinks in India is around five to

> A food product that is categorized as the topmost junk food by health experts is in fact the biggest success story of the Ministry of Food Processing Industries.

six bottles, compared to Pakistan's seventeen, Sri Lanka's twenty-one, Thailand's seventy-three, the Philippines' 173 and Mexico's 605. Therefore, the ministry would like see the Indian market grow 'at twice the rate of GDP growth.'[17]

With a sense of pride and achievement, the ministry informs that 'soft and aerated drinks were considered products for the middle class and the affluent. That segregation is no longer valid. Soft and aerated drinks are consumed by all except those who cannot afford to buy any drink.' Now you know why soft drinks have become an essential part of every fridge. The MFPI quotes a study done by the National Council for Applied Economic Research to point out that '91 per cent of soft drink sales are made to the lower, middle and upper middle classes.'[18] This has prompted the industry to demand the removal of special excise duty.

Colas and sugary drinks are being positioned as basic mass consumed items like water and tea and not something you drink only in summer. Both Coke and Pepsi are targeting movie halls, malls and eateries to boost what they call 'in-home' or 'in-premise' consumption so that sales are not impacted by the weather. 'Around 90 per cent of all beverages (tea, milk, water etc.) is consumed at home or the indoors because you have meals at home, work in office and spend weekends in a restaurant or a cinema hall. Fifteen years ago, in-home consumption of soft drinks was only 10 per cent. In 2011, it was 40 per cent,' a Coca-Cola executive said in a media interview.[19]

In accordance with the MFPI's dream of catalyzing a double-digit growth of the cola market, cola companies are aggressively targeting rural consumers with special, low-priced products. Coke has designed a new product, 'Fanta Fun Taste', a powder that can be mixed with water and consumed. Pepsi began marketing in 2011, at Rs 5, an 'energy drink' called Gluco+

Colas and sugary drinks are being positioned as basic mass consumed items like water and tea and not something you drink only in summer.

to address 'the need gap of health and energy' of rural people. 'A large number of them are daily wage earners. So the key is to remain fit (in order) to not lose their daily income,' and this is the company's logic behind the push it is giving to the product.[20] Coke even feels that cola is as essential as drinking water. 'Every human being needs 2 litres of fluid per day. We see a lot of opportunity as the consumers there (in rural areas) too have a right to choice and products we consume in cities. So the opportunity and the challenge is how we take that great taste in beverages to people who can afford to spend Rs 3–5,' a Coke executive said, explaining his company's rural thrust.[21] The Brown Revolution is indeed reaching India's grassroots.

State Support to Junk Food

Traditionally, agriculture and farming communities were the cornerstones of India's food policies. With the founding of the MFPI and the subsequent opening up of the economy, the policy focus shifted to the food supply chain – processors, traders, retailers, marketers. This was a fundamental change.

The approval of the Pepsi project in 1988 was followed by the decision to allow import of oilseeds and seeds of pulses, cereals, vegetables and flowers by traders, big farmers or anyone else in the seed business. Post-harvest processing of farm produce was known as 'agro-business' in official jargon till then and was part of the functions of the Ministry of Food and Agriculture. Keeping in mind administrative difficulties that had been faced in getting the Pepsi proposal approved, Rajiv Gandhi created a new government department called the Ministry of Food Processing Industries (MFPI) in July 1988. Its objective was to provide a link between the farmer and

> The food processing industry – till then reserved for small-scale units – was thrown open for big industries and the import of food processing equipment was liberalized.

the industry to ensure 'better utilization of agriculture products, greater value addition to rural produce, enhancement of net levels of rural incomes and induction of modern technology into food processing'.[22] To begin with, the food processing industry – till then reserved for small-scale units – was thrown open for big industries and the import of food processing equipment was liberalized.

While the new outfit was claimed to have been created to help the farmers, the 'allocation of business', which defines the actual role of a ministry in the Indian administrative system, stated something different: 'Planning, development and control of, and assistance to, industries relating to bread, oilseeds, breakfast foods, biscuits, confectionary, chocolate making, malt extract, protein isolates, high-protein foods, weaning food and extruded food products (including other ready-to-eat foods)'.[23] Over the years, the MFPI's role was expanded to cover the 'cereal-based consumer food industry, which includes pasta, breads, cakes, pastries, rusks, buns, rolls, noodles, rice flakes, corn flakes, biscuits, ready-to-eat and ready-to-cook products etc.,' and to provide 'financial assistance for setting up/modernization/expansion of the consumer food industries'.[24] Beer, wine and alcoholic drinks from a non-molasses base have also been included in this list.

In effect, the government has taken upon itself the task of actively 'stimulating demand for processed food'. Within two decades of the MFPI being set up, it has transformed itself into a major state-supported mechanism to promote processed foods. The Indian State provides direct financial grants, soft loans and concessional credit to set up new processed food units as well as to refurbish the existing ones. Tax concessions of a wide range have been made available to food processors. Subsidies are being doled out to develop infrastructural facilities, such as food parks, quality testing laboratories, research and development units, training

> The MFPI even airs radio jingles and releases newspaper ads to tell people that processed food is 'safe, convenient and healthy'.

institutes and entrepreneurship development programmes for the benefit of the food industry.

The State even funds market research studies, surveys, seminars and exhibitions to promote junk food. Doles are also given to industry associations. In 2010–11, the ministry provided financial support to organizers of 113 industry conferences and towards promotion of food processing. The MFPI even airs radio jingles and releases newspaper ads to tell people that processed food is 'safe, convenient and healthy'. One of the chief objectives of the ministry is to 'facilitate the creation of a conducive environment for healthy growth of the food processing sector'. Billions and billions of rupees are doled out every year by the State as subsidies and grants to private industry and are spent in promoting unhealthy junk food.

Most of the processed food products have been exempted from industrial licensing. There is no cap on FDI in all food processing sectors. Companies making several categories of processed food products enjoy exemption from income tax. Excise duty on pasta, ice creams, ready-to-eat packaged foods, biscuits and instant mixes has been waived off. The MFPI has set up the Indian Grape Processing Board to promote a 'sustainable growth of the wine sector'. The Board wants Indians to appreciate 'the fine art of wine drinking' and position Indian wine as 'an alternative to hard liquor'.[25]

Under a scheme called 'technology upgradation, modernization and setting up of food processing industries', anybody interested in starting a food processing unit for biscuits, potato chips, cakes, pastries, instant mixes, noodles, pastas or namkeen can get grants of 25 per cent of the cost of plant and machinery and 'technical civil works', subject to a maximum of Rs 50 lakh in 'general' areas and 33.3 per cent or Rs 75 lakh in 'difficult' areas. Similar liberal grants are available for existing food processing

> Billions and billions of rupees are doled out as subsidies and grants to private industry and are spent in promoting unhealthy junk food every year by the State.

units wishing to upgrade their processes or modernize. The list of grantees runs into several hundreds and includes big companies such as Rasna Private Limited and Marico Limited.[26] During the Twelfth Plan period, the ministry proposes to provide subsidies to the food industry to the tune of Rs 10,300 crore in the form of 'capital assistance'. Promoters of mega food parks can get a subsidy of Rs 50 crore for each park. Over Rs 3200 crore will be given away as subsidy for such parks during 2012 and 2017.

Government schemes are aimed at encouraging farmers to diversify into horticulture. The area under cultivation of such crops (fruits and vegetables, flowers, nuts, spices, aromatic and medicinal plants, mushroom, honey and plantation crops) has seen a 62 per cent growth between 1991–92 and 2008–09, while the area under pulses dipped by 1 per cent and that under cereals rose by just 2 per cent during the same year. Data about consumption as reflected in the Monthly Per Capita Expenditure (MPCE) report shows that consumption of cereals declined by 6 per cent in rural areas and 4 per cent in urban areas during the period between 1999–2000 and 2007–08, while consumption of high-value crops including fruits and vegetables grew by 3 per cent in rural areas and 1 per cent in urban areas during the same period.[27] This means, while the production of horticultural crops has gone up substantially, their domestic consumption has not grown proportionately. A bulk of the increased production of horticultural crops has been consumed by exports.

Growing more fruits and vegetables is a good step as it could improve the nutritional status of the malnourished. Fruit and vegetable production is on the rise but it is not helping in bringing about a change in the nutrition levels of the poor. With the expansion and sophisticated retail marketing, affordable supply of fruits and vegetables may have gone up in urban areas, but the availability and access to fruits and vegetables in rural areas is much more limited, a study done in Asian countries, including India, concluded in 2009. This is because mainly cash crops are being

The 'horticulture' basket is growing but it contains more of cash crops meant solely for export. Policies expressly support exports through grants, subsidies, market promotion activities and promotion of schemes.

produced for export and sale. 'Fruits and vegetables in supermarkets and larger markets may appear to be cheaper than smaller local food stores or markets, but when the cost of individual travel to the stores is included, the difference is negligible,' the study noted.[28] The 'horticulture' basket is growing but it contains more of cash crops meant solely for export. Policies expressly support exports through grants, subsidies, market promotion activities and promotion of schemes like agri export zones. Diversion of agricultural lands to grow flowers in order to cater to 'the cut flower' markets in Europe is an example of this new export thrust.

At a time when health experts are suggesting the promotion of freshly cooked food and food diversity to prevent a plethora of lifestyle diseases, the MFPI is listing 'socio-cultural factors such as the preference of Indians for freshly plucked/cooked food, variation in food habits across the country, easy availability of raw materials for cooking and preference for consumption of food at home' as constraints for the food processing sector in India.[29] So, all efforts being made with the tax payers' money are directed at overcoming these hurdles. Agricultural production, in its view, is mere 'raw material for food processing'. Public funds are being used to promote processed food, which nutritionists and doctors consider unhealthy.

Votaries of food processing argue that it is good for farmers as it helps even out seasonal peaks and troughs in prices and checks waste. In addition, growth of the food processing sector helps achieve increased agricultural production by ensuring better remuneration for farmers as well as better access to markets. Value-addition generates additional employment and export earnings, which, in turn, lead to better socio-economic conditions of millions of farm families.[30] All these are valid arguments in principle, but there is little evidence to prove that subsidies being doled out by the MFPI are indeed resulting in such benefits to farmers. Most of the subsidies are flowing to rice mills, bakeries, biscuit companies, beverage makers, wineries and other food processing industries, as reflected in the MFPI data. Beer, wine, cola and milk are all being treated in a similar fashion by the benign state, because they fall in the category of processed foods and are supposed to help farmers. Nearly two decades of subsidies and grants have hardly been able to completely prevent a massive waste of perishable fruits and vegetables, which is often touted as the justification for the support the State extends to processors.

Polished Rice, Palm Oil and Politics

Rice, one of the staple foods of Indians, is a classic case of how state and corporate policies are working in tandem to adversely impact the health of Indians. While health experts consider polished rice to be one of the main factors leading to the rise in diabetes cases, the government is busy promoting the rice milling industry in a big way. Paddy has to be milled in order to remove husk and impurities, but commercial rice mills make paddy go through intense processing in order to produce white rice.

In 1997, the government repealed the Rice Milling Industry (Regulation) Act, 1958, doing away with the mandatory government permission for setting up new rice mills. The number of rice mills jumped to 125,000 within ten years.[31] The MFPI subsidizes milling of rice, wheat and pulses. Rice millers can get cash grants of up to Rs 75 lakh towards the purchase of plant and machinery as well as construction of the building. All this is geared to bring more processed flour, rice and pulses into the market.

> Public funds are being used to promote processed food, which nutritionists and doctors consider unhealthy.

Rice loses its fibre, vitamin, magnesium and other mineral content when it is processed.

A group of American and Japanese researchers reported in 2010 that brown rice (the least processed form of rice) fares better than the white or polished variety because it offers protection from high blood pressure and thickening of the arteries.[32] A component in a layer of tissue surrounding grains of brown rice may work against angiotensin II – an endocrine protein and a known culprit in the development of high blood pressure and atherosclerosis. When brown rice is polished to make it white, the sub-aleurone layer is stripped away and the rice loses some of its nutrients. The sub-aleurone layer can be preserved in half-milled rice or incompletely milled rice.

White or milled rice has also been linked to an increased risk of diabetes. In June 2010, researchers from the Harvard School of Public Health reported that eating five or more servings of white rice per week was associated with an increased risk of Type 2 diabetes.[33] In contrast, eating two or more servings of brown rice per week was associated with a lower risk of the disease. The researchers estimated that replacing 50 grams of white rice (just one-third of a typical daily serving) with the same amount of brown rice would lower the risk of Type 2 diabetes by 16 per cent. The same replacement with other whole grains, such as whole wheat and barley, was associated with a 36 per cent reduced risk. This means that the subsidies given for rice milling are actually state funding in order to promote the key risk factors of heart disease.

Dr V. Mohan has conducted a study on rice consumption in Chennai. He divided population groups based on their rice intake – going up from 100 gm to 400 gm of rice every day. He noticed that prevalence of diabetes exactly quadruples as rice consumption increases from 100 to 400 gm. This was after accounting for other factors like physical activity, family history, obesity etc. This, Dr Mohan says, means the rice intake is independently contributing to diabetes.[34] People may think there is nothing wrong with rice consumption since they have been eating the same rice for centuries. Dr Mohan said, 'The rice which was consumed in the 1970s was not milled, it was hand pounded, it was brownish, had more fibre and protein. Polishing removes the outer bran and the rice becomes thinner. If the government says highly polished rice will be taxed more – just like tobacco – it will become costly and people may start buying brown rice.'[35]

The free import policy pursued by the government helped flood the Indian markets with cheap palm oil, ignoring growing scientific evidence that this oil is bad for the heart.

The edible oil story is no different. Soon after the process of trade liberalization began in India, import curbs on edible oil were removed in order to meet shortages. Despite accounting for 9.3 per cent of world oilseed production, about 43 per cent of edible oil in India is imported.[36] Between 1994 and 2000, import duties were slashed on both refined and non-refined oils progressively from 65 per cent to 15 per cent. In 2008, duty on refined oil was 7.5 per cent and there was no duty on raw or unrefined oil. Free imports meant that refined oil could be imported, packed and distributed without the need of having a manufacturing facility locally. As a result, the vegetable oil scenario in India completely changed by the end of the 1990s. Palm oil, which accounted for just 4 per cent of calories available from all vegetable oils in 1989–91, was contributing to 28 per cent of calories in 2000–02. This was in contrast to the situation in the 1970s, when domestically produced peanut, rapeseed and cottonseed oils dominated.[37]

The free import policy pursued by the government helped flood the Indian markets with cheap palm oil, ignoring growing scientific evidence that this oil is bad for the heart. The decision was mainly driven by economic considerations and greatly influenced by the powerful palm oil lobby of South East Asia.

Palm oil is derived from the pulp of fruits of the oil palms. In contrast to the palm oil industry's contentions, leading health authorities – supported by medical research on the health effects of different fats – agree that palm oil promotes heart disease.[38] Two meta-analyses, which combine similar studies to achieve greater statistical strength, have examined the effect of palmitic acid on serum cholesterol. The first one, based on 134 human experiments, concluded that palmitic acid raises the blood cholesterol levels.[39] The second study done in 2003 reported that palmitic acid increases the ratio of total cholesterol to HDL cholesterol, an important indicator of heart disease risk, more than other saturated fatty acids. The WHO believes there is 'convincing evidence' that palmitic acid increases the risk of cardiovascular disease.[40]

Regulation of trans-fatty acids (TFA) is another area where the State has been wavering. Trans-fats, which lower good cholesterol and boost bad ones, are also added artificially in blended oils and vanaspati used in making most bakery products and namkeen. A major part of TFA in Indian diets is derived from partially hydrogenated vegetable oils. Considering the role TFA plays in the development of heart disease, the WHO, in September 2006, recommended the phasing out of artificial trans-fats from all foods. The Indian health ministry failed to act despite a recommendation from one of its own wings – Edible Oils and Fats Subcommittee of the Central Committee on Food Safety (CCFS) – to limit the use of TFAs. In January 2008, the subcommittee forwarded its recommendations to the Central Committee for Standards with a detailed plan to phase out TFAs. But instead of setting standards for TFAs in cooking oils, the ministry in September 2008 issued a notification for labelling of trans-fats on oil packages and food.

Merely putting the TFA content on labels – without fixing an upper limit – served little purpose as exposed by the Centre for Science and Environment (CSE) – a Delhi-based environment action group – in January 2009. It found that all vanaspati brands whose trans-fat levels were tested had five to twelve times higher TFA content than the world's only standard for trans-fats in oil, set in Denmark, at 2 per cent of the total oil. But the government did not budge beyond labelling. Health minister A. Ramadoss ruled out taking any drastic measure (such as banning TFAs) 'because proper substitutes would have to be looked into and it had to be kept in mind that the price of vegetable oil was a highly politically sensitive issue'.[41]

The trans-fats episode, once again, demonstrated that the government – and the health ministry – is fully aware of the dangers trans-fats pose to heart disease. Yet it is not willing to take tough measures due to political limitations.

'Burgerization' of Food

One of the earliest post-liberalization trends noticed in the Indian food market was the emergence of packaged food. Instead of buying farm produce on a quarterly or yearly basis or unpackaged groceries from local stores on a daily or weekly basis, people started buying food items every month or fortnight from supermarkets or convenience stores. The practice of buying whole wheat and getting it ground in a neighbourhood mill gave way to packaged and branded flour. Ready-to-eat or pre-cooked foods were the next ones to hit the market in a big way. Frozen and canned foods that can be heated and served instantly have gained a permanent place on the kitchen shelves of middle class Indians. Maggi has become almost an iconic brand of this segment of the food market, which now includes a range of items catering to different regional tastes – from Kashmiri pulao to Chettinad chicken. The noodles market, said to be worth almost Rs 3500 crore a year, is growing at a rate of 20 to 25 per cent a year. Companies estimate that a typical Indian family consumes 20 to 25 packets of noodles every year.[42] Most television commercials position noodles as a 'mini-meal' and are targeted at children. Almost every street corner in Indian cities sells some form of noodles. Overall, the ready-to-eat market in India, which was estimated to be worth Rs 128 crore in 2006, is projected to

One of the earliest post-liberalization trends noticed in the Indian food market was the emergence of packaged food.

grow to Rs 2900 crore by 2015, mainly driven by factors like rising disposable incomes, diminishing culinary skills and growing need for convenience.[43]

Eating out assumed a new meaning in the post-liberalization period. In 2013, it was reported that Indians were eating out as many as seven times a month. Perhaps the most visible face of globalization are fast-food outlets run by multinational corporations – mostly American – such as McDonald's and Pizza Hut – which dot main thoroughfares of all major Indian cities. Kentucky Fried Chicken and Taco Bell – owned by Yum! Brands, Inc., which also owns Pizza Hut – are other fast-food chains which have opened outlets in the country. Yum! announced its plans to have 500 KFC outlets in place by 2015.[44] In August 2012, Domino's opened its 500th store in India and projected to have another 100 by March 2013.[45] McDonald's, which had 271 outlets in India by mid-2012, brands itself as 'McDonald's Family Restaurants' in a marketing strategy to position itself as a family outing place. In June 2009, Amit Jatia, a company official said, 'People in India are used to McDonald's and are now starting to rely on it as it becomes more than just the occasional treat for India's increasingly affluent middle class.'[46]

The Rs 9000-crore 'organized eating out' market in India is said to be growing at 25 per cent a year.[47] In March 2011, the *Financial Times* reported that sales at Western fast-food chains and their local rivals in India are growing at an average of 28 per cent a year. Indians spent an estimated $1.3 billion on dining out in 'chain restaurants' in 2009, of which about $400 million was accounted for by fast food, according to the research group Euromonitor.[48] Besides pre-cooked food products and fast-food restaurants, the Indian snacking industry has seen tremendous growth in the post-liberalization years. Snacking has always been a part of the Indian way of life. It is common practice in different parts of the country to offer a stored salted snack – namkeen – or a freshly cooked one such as a pakora, samosa or kachori.

Food marketing has been widely recognized as an effective tool to influence food choice, and is considered an independent cause behind changing dietary patterns.

Liberalization policies have given birth to a branded segment of the Indian snacking industry now estimated to be worth Rs 3000 crore. Bikaneri Bhujia – a generic name given to snacks produced in Bikaner – tops the list of traditional branded snacks with an annual turnover of about Rs 1000 crore.[49] Marketers say they are catering to the changing eating habits of urban Indians who are devoting less time to a full meal but are eating more frequently. Instead of three main meals, now there are six 'snacking occasions', which food companies are targeting.[50]

All across urban India, marketers are noticing the same 'snacking and grazing' consumption behaviour prevalent in developed countries. Portable snack foods are becoming a ready substitute for hot snacks as consumers are moving towards more cosmopolitan lifestyles.[51] Companies are also reaching out to low-income groups in cities and people in the rural areas. Noodle companies are specifically targeting urban slums and rural areas with smaller packs costing just Rs 5. Tiny packs of a variety of bakery items – costing Rs 5 – are being pushed into rural markets. 'Me too' versions of noodles, burgers, pizzas and such items – introduced by fast-food chains such as McDonald's – are now available as street food.

Food Marketing Drives Dietary Change

Food marketing has been widely recognized as an effective tool to influence food choice, and is considered an independent cause behind changing dietary patterns. The advertising budgets of food companies, fast-food restaurant chains and beverage makers are constantly going up all over the world. Coke and McDonald's are said to be among the top ten corporate advertisers globally. Just like free trade and FDI, marketing is also a process of globalization. It is 'a self-reinforcing process: just as marketing facilitates globalization, globalization facilitates marketing.'[52]

Advertising is necessary to enable the consumer make a choice from an array of products. In the case of food products, critics point out, it would be an exaggeration to say that each individual's choice somehow develops on the basis of a full and rational knowledge of a product.[53] Very few consumers may be making informed choices based on the actual features – nutrient value, health impact or ecological footprint – of commodities. Consumers are being offered an array of branded products that actually differ very little from each other. Companies highlight these minor differences to create brand loyalties by associating their products with a certain lifestyle or with emotions (like love, affection, happiness, joy, care, bravery etc.) through advertising. Non-material needs are sought to be met by material products. Food companies are devising persuasive advertising and marketing messages in a manner similar to tobacco advertising in its initial years.

Food marketing extends beyond advertising of biscuits, colas, chips and pizzas. It involves designing strategies and activities that influence consumption habits and create demand. It can take myriad forms: hoardings, newspaper ads, television commercials, sales promotion websites, sponsorship of events, contests, in-school marketing, point-of-purchase ads, co-branding, interactive games on the internet, fan pages on social networks and product placements in television serials and films. The expansion of media has placed newer tools of advertising in the hands of marketers. The process of globalization of diets has been complemented by the globalization of media. There are nearly 500 television channels in Hindi, English and regional languages. Besides providing avenues for advertising, satellite television, much like Hollywood movies, has also exposed Indians to the Western ways of living and food habits. 'When rural people see pizzas and burgers being advertised on television, their expectations rise and they are only waiting for the same stuff to come to villages,' said Dr Mohan.[54]

> Food marketing extends beyond advertising of biscuits, colas, chips and pizzas. It involves designing strategies and activities that influence consumption habits and create demand.

Advertising of food products is mostly targeted at children because it is believed that food tastes and habits developed during childhood are difficult to get over later on in life. Food multinationals are targeting the bulk of their advertising at children. Ads of colas, chips, noodles and such products project children in different roles. In 2006, a WHO panel concluded that exposure to the promotion of energy-dense, nutrient-poor foods and beverages can adversely affect children's eating habits.[55] The marketing is more for energy-dense, micronutrient-poor foods, which completely undermines the recommendations for a healthy diet. The WHO says advertising has an adverse effect on children's understanding of food, purchase behaviour and consumption. In addition to their dietary habits, food marketing influences nutrition knowledge and food preferences of children.[56]

The foods advertised on television tend to oversupply nutrients associated with chronic illness (saturated fat, cholesterol, and sodium) and undersupply nutrients that help protect against illness (fibre, vitamins A, E, and D, calcium, and potassium).[57] Children exposed to junk food spots on television reported a greater desire as well as preference for sweet and fatty food.[58]

In April 2010, children's television channels bombarded viewers with 44,887 commercials of processed food, according to the industry research firm, What's On Television. Kids watching television after school – between 4 to 6 p.m. – were exposed to twenty-one ads of processed foods every day.[59] Nick India reported a 70 per cent growth in its ad revenues during the fiscal year 2010, and a bulk of it came from food companies, Nestlé and GSK.[60] The total number of brands advertised on the channel were 309. 'Food and Beverages' was the most advertised sector on television in 2010, contributing 14 per cent to the overall television advertising pie. In the first half of 2011, this category witnessed a 10 per cent growth, clocking a total of 18,009 hours in six months. Aerated soft drinks were the most advertised within 'Food and Beverages', followed by milk beverages, chocolates, biscuits, non-aerated soft drinks, tea, noodles and pasta, chewing gum and edible oil. Ten per cent of all food and beverages advertising went to kids' channels.[61]

It is not just the food companies which are advertising. The Indian government feels that it is its duty to seriously promote junk food as a generic category of products. A series of print ads released by the MFPI in newspapers in 2010 made a shocking proclamation: 'Processed foods are as healthy as fresh fruits'. 'Processed foods,' the ad issued by the MFPI proclaimed, 'are just as nutritious or in some cases more nutritious than fresh foods depending on the manner in which they are processed.' The ads also depicted two animated characters called 'better quality' and 'better health'. Another MFPI ad in the series asks consumers to 'change your thought towards nutrition in processed foods'. It says processed foods are good for health because 'any food item processed with superlative technology stands second to none in purity, freshness and nutrition, which is just right for your health.' Then it goes on to list good qualities of junk food as 'quality and preservative tested for health, manufactured under hygienic conditions, untouched by hand, adulteration prevented, more shelf life, very convenient, more testier (sic).'

A random analysis of television commercials and print ads of food products showed that they weave emotional, persuasive family stories to project packaged and pre-cooked, energy-dense food to be superior to or a substitute for home-cooked and fresh food. For instance, one depicts noodles as a favourite dish for children after play, while another shows that the child who carries pre-cooked food

A series of print ads released by the MFPI in newspapers in 2010 made a shocking proclamation: 'Processed foods are as healthy as fresh fruits'.

in his tiffin box to school is treated with respect by his peers. Still others portray how young housewives can serve their husbands and children 'fresh' food in a jiffy with the help of ready-to-eat food mixes. Such foods, the ads assure the viewers, taste as good as grandma's cooking. A television spot of Domino's Pizza positions pizza as a smart replacement of home-cooked lunch supplied by the famous dabbawalas in Mumbai. All ads position processed, packaged and ready-to-eat food as a 'healthy and nutritious' substitute for home-cooked, fresh and traditional foods.

With such spots, the food industry is targeting the cultural values of people. Food is an integral part of the Indian tradition and culture, and the culinary skills are supposed to be carried forward through generations. This chain is sought to be broken by food companies that want to position themselves as purveyors of traditional cooking knowledge and skills. It is not just the question of who the custodian of cooking skills and knowledge is – grandma or the food industry – but 'why are cooking skills important'. While the food industry and its proponents may argue that pre-cooked and ultra processed food liberates women from the drudgery of traditional cooking, others feel, 'when not being taught how to cook, people lose the basic means of taking control of their diets'. People cannot be expected to be in full control of their diets – as nutritionists and health educators would like them to – if they do not know what goes into the food or they do not know cooking at all. If people start depending on others or the food industry provides it for them, it is feared, it would give rise to a culture of dependency.[62]

Luring kids with freebies, gifts or free tickets to cricket matches is the mainstay of food marketing. The Happy Meals of McDonald's, which usually combine burger and fries with colas, has popularized a series of toys that go with it. In the US, such combo

The Happy Meals of McDonald's, which usually combine burger and fries with colas, has popularized a series of toys that go with it.

All nutritional and health benefit claims should be substantiated scientifically. Also, unless a food product has been nutritionally designed as a meal replacement, it should not be portrayed as such.

offers like free toys with fast-food meals and soda sizes have begun to attract regulatory restrictions. Food companies also indulge in direct marketing to children through schools. Hindustan Unilever launched a direct marketing drive to push Knorr Soupy Noodles towards school children in January 2011 to 'promote the product as a fun-filled, healthy snack'.[63] Another noodle maker, Nissin, organized a special 'consumer engagement activity' for children and mothers to 'educate them about the right method of preparing instant noodles' because 'the taste of noodles depends on the way we cook it'.[64] In 2011, PepsiCo launched an 'education programme' for school kids in ninety-five villages to test market its low-priced snack Lehar Iron Chusti because the company believes girls are not aware that they suffer from anaemia. Along with 'health education', the company sneaked in the message, 'how Chusti can help supplement the dietary regime'.[65]

Currently, no restrictions are in place on food advertising aimed at children, despite the WHO guidance given in 2004 to governments, industry and consumers to take action against marketing messages that promote unhealthy dietary practices. The Indian government has merely recognized a self-regulatory code of Advertising Standards Council of India (ASCI), which talks of broad principles such as truthfulness and honesty.[66] In 2007, ASCI issued 'self-regulation guidelines on the advertising of foods and beverages directed at children under thirteen years of age', recognizing that 'caution and care should be observed in advertising of foods and beverages, especially the ones containing relatively high fat, sugar and salt'. Advertisements should not mislead consumers about personal changes in intelligence, physical ability or exceptional recognition. All nutritional and health benefit claims should be substantiated scientifically. Also, unless a food product has been nutritionally designed as a meal replacement, it should not be portrayed as such. Advertisements should not show overconsumption of foods and beverages. Adherence to this code is voluntary.

The problem with self-regulation is that it does not actually prohibit or restrict the volume of food marketing to children. The India Pledge announced by seven food and beverages companies in July 2010 is a case in point.[67] The participating companies (Coca-Cola, General Mills, Kellogg, Nestlé, Mars, PepsiCo and Hindustan Unilever) pledged to implement 'company-specific voluntary measures on food and beverage advertising to children' by December 2010. They pledged not to advertise 'food and beverage products to children under the age of twelve on TV, print or the Internet, except for products that fulfil specific nutrition criteria based on accepted scientific evidence and/or applicable national and international dietary guidelines'. Cola companies claim that none of their products are unhealthy. This means they can continue to advertise like before. 'Advertising to children under twelve years' was defined as 'advertising to media audiences where at least half are children under the age of twelve'. Nobody knows how one determines audiences where 50 per cent of the viewers are below twelve. Similarly, companies said they would not engage in 'any commercial communications related to food and beverage products in primary schools' except where 'specifically requested by or agreed by the school administration for educational purposes'.

Such voluntary actions actually leave the door wide open for both advertising and promotion targeted at children. Only statutory regulations that aim to reduce the intensity of marketing for energy-dense, nutrient-poor foods clearly targeted at children could be useful. Regulations should limit food marketing to children in specific places, times and techniques (in specific settings such as schools, specific to periods of time when children are particularly exposed to marketing, or when they are watching television programmes, and specific to techniques widely used to target children, such as free gifts and collectables). Film and cricket celebrities are roped in as brand ambassadors to advertise soft drinks and junk food. Some experts have advocated nutritional warnings for imbalanced foods similar to those mandated on direct-to-consumer drug advertisements.

A related issue is that of food labelling that can be a means to enable consumers to make a healthy choice while purchasing a food product. Regulations in different countries require manufacturers to print information about ingredients along with basic information like price and weight. Nutritional labelling has also been made mandatory in many countries including India. While nutritional labelling on product packs has been made mandatory, manufacturers have been allowed to make health-related claims in advertising since there are no codes or restrictions on advertising of junk foods on television or in print. In every television commercial of a processed food product – be it noodles, pasta, pickles, cookies, cheese, cooking oil – the imagery and the message are designed to portray that it is a 'healthier substitute' for home-made and traditional food. Instead of formulating strict regulations to curb such practices, the Food Safety and Standards Authority of India (FSSAI) in 2013 unveiled a plan to legitimize such claims by deciding to allow wide-ranging 'disease-risk-reduction' claims on food products.[68]

The 'healthy' tags on junk food products are misleading and farcical. When the Ahmedabad-based agency Consumer Education and Research Centre tested some leading brands of noodles for their health claims, it found that most brands were high on sodium and low on fibre contrary to the claims they were making. They had minuscule amounts of iron, calcium and other minerals that would hardly add any nutritional value as claimed in the advertisements. Even if the claims made are technically correct, they have no health impact. 'For instance,' says endocrinologist Dr Anoop Misra, 'it is a myth that if a label claims the product is "cholesterol free" then it would not affect blood cholesterol. He says even if a product has zero grams of cholesterol it can still negatively affect blood cholesterol as it contains other ingredients like trans- or saturated fats (which raise bad cholesterol).'[69] A 2008 study of breakfast cereals by Consumers International in thirty-two countries including India found claims made by companies like Kellogg and Nestlé about salt, sugar and fat content of their cereals to be false.[70] Even the information given on labels was incorrect. For instance, the label on Kellogg 's heavily advertised cereal, Chocos, mentioned that it contained 23.3 grams of sugar per 100 grams of cereal, but laboratory tests showed that it contained 32.8 grams. The study concluded that most cereals had 'more sugar than a doughnut' and were 'as salty as seawater'.

> Food companies deploy public relations firms to promote 'corporate science' related to health, food and environment issues, and to create a smokescreen of social responsibility.

In a desperate bid to go 'healthy', food companies are aggressively hiring institutions run by health professionals to endorse their products. Some of them are floating their own medical bodies solely for endorsements and 'education campaigns'. PepsiCo crossed all ethical boundaries in the endorsement game by signing up with the Indian Medical Association (IMA), a professional body of Indian doctors, to put its seal of approval on some of its non-carbonated sugary drinks. The doctors' body was paid Rs 1.56 crore for the endorsement. Besides endorsing Tropicana fruit juice and Quaker Oats of PepsiCo, IMA also got funds from the soft-drink maker for its Continuing Medical Education programmes (CMEs). When Dr Babu K.V., a member of the IMA, dragged the matter to the Medical Council of India (MCI), whose rules prohibit product endorsements by doctors, it refused to take any action against the IMA, saying that its regulations did not cover professional bodies like this. Only towards the end of the three-year contract in 2010 did MCI hold that the IMA endorsement was unethical.[71] Food companies deploy public relations firms to promote 'corporate science' related to health, food and environment issues, and to create a smokescreen of social responsibility. Companies float organizations with credible sounding names to spread the 'right' information relating to the food industry and its products.

Nutrition Institute, floated by Nestlé, is another example. This body routinely organizes or sponsors 'scientific conferences' where paid experts talk about nutrition while fitting in Nestlé products in their recommendations. The Association of Adolescent Child Care in India (AACCI) is yet another example of a corporate science outfit. This body, supported fully by Hindustan Unilever, organized a National Child Health Summit in Greater Noida in 2009, and instituted the National Child Health Awards.[72] Britannia Nutrition Foundation is another industry-promoted body that is trying to position unhealthy processed foods as a panacea for malnutrition. It is ironical that an industry that vehemently denies that its products cause adverse health impacts is now trying so desperately to position its products as 'healthy' and provide consumers with, what it calls, healthy choices.

Food Industry as the Policy and Standard Maker

The formulation of food policies – encompassing everything from production to consumption – is a complex process and a highly contested arena. The first set of players in this game are government agencies – ministries of food, agriculture, food supplies, health and environment. Several other wings of the government are involved in this process indirectly. Their actions, in effect, act as building blocks of the food policy. For instance, the commerce ministry is formulating a segment of the food policy while deciding trade policies or the finance ministry may be doing so when it tinkers with import duties or fiscal incentives. Their decisions – though trade and fiscal-related – can change dietary patterns, nutrition intake and increase the risk of heart disease. Similarly, the urban development ministry and local planning boards are contributing to food policy while making decisions relating to shortlisting of the location/sites for construction of supermarkets and malls.

It is clear from the narrative that the Indian State, through its policies, is actively engaged in promoting the food processing industry by extending tax concessions, tax breaks, creating markets, helping in exports and even offering liberal cash grants. On the other hand, it has turned a blind eye to health concerns and hasn't shown any interest in introducing measures to discourage the consumption of junk foods that is directly linked to obesity, diabetes and cardiovascular diseases, or to promote consumption of healthy food items.

A major player in food policymaking is the corporate sector or the food industry. With every new product or marketing strategy, the food industry is, in effect, deciding the food policy. For instance, 'when the food industry sets specifications for its food products, it actually determines the nutritional intake of consumers.'[73] Food companies in India are selling specific products to people of the rural areas which supposedly contain micro-nutrients, thereby writing the nutrition policies for those areas. When Pepsi launches an 'energy drink' to address 'the need gap of health and energy' of the rural people in India, it will be doing the same thing. Just consider the rationale given by a PepsiCo executive for introducing a low-priced biscuit for rural women: 'Opportunity mapping gave us an insight that 55 per cent of Indian women are anaemic. And the point of intervention is when you are an adolescent or when you are a mother. We chose the former.' This, in effect, means that the food company is deciding a policy based on the health conditions of the people and the interventions needed to address them – a function so far under the Ministry of Health. The same corporate entity takes another nutrition policy decision for rural Indians – they need extra sugar and electrolytes – because it wants to introduce a new 'dissolve and drink' beverage called Gluco+ for them.[74]

Similarly, if Coke decides that you should consume its aerated drinks all year round – and not just during summer – and also drink it more often at home and not just when you go out, it is setting the food policy for a class of people and is deciding that people should increase their sugar intake. Eggs have become a part of the Indian diet not because nutritionists felt that Indians need more protein or because research found deficiencies linked to lack of egg consumption. Egg intake went up because one poultry industry – Venkateswara – decided that Indians should eat eggs every day, thereby increasing their protein, fat and cholesterol intake. (Egg yolks contain 213 milligrams of cholesterol and 5 grams of total fat including saturated fat which increases blood cholesterol levels, but the Venkateswara-sponsored National Egg Coordination Committee in its TV commercials – which exhort people to consume eggs everyday – does not mention such facts). This amounted to a major policy decision relating to nutrition.

The food industry is not only setting health, nutrition and food policies this way, it is also influencing policymaking within the state apparatus. Industry organizations such as the Federation of Indian Chambers of Commerce and Industry (FICCI) and Confederation of Indian Industry (CII) are 'closely involved while developing the programmes of the food processing ministry and (in) their implementation.'[75]

Regulation, which is an exclusive domain of the State or the regulators appointed by it, too has not been saved from industry influence. The food industry infiltrated the scientific panels of even the Indian food regulatory system. The list of industry men appointed on the scientific panels of the FSSAI in 2009 read like a virtual who's who of the global and Indian food industry – PepsiCo, Coca-Cola, Hindustan Unilever, GSK Healthcare, Britannia, Marico, ITC and Nestlé.[76] In an apparent case of the regulated becoming the regulators themselves, the array of scientific panels were packed with industry representatives who were supposed to provide 'scientific opinion' to the food authority on a range of critical issues like labelling, food additives, pesticide residues, genetically

A complex state-industry nexus is responsible for the changing food environment in favour of unhealthy foods.

modified food and even decide on methods of sampling and analysis. Following exposure in the press, the matter was included in an ongoing case in the Supreme Court, which, in February 2011, ordered that the authority be purged of all industry nominees.[77]

Industry participation in its standard setting and regulation process continued even after the SC rap. The food industry was represented in key official panels dealing with food standards under the aegis of FSSAI. Known as Shadow Committees of the National Codex Committees, these panels prepare the official stand of the Indian government for international negotiations on food standards held by the Codex Alimentarius Commission – a joint forum of the WHO and the Food and Agriculture Organization (FAO). Publicly available minutes of Codex meetings show that food industry officials, such as those from Nestlé and GSK, routinely represent India as official delegates in Codex negotiations, clearly overlooking conflicts of interest. The industry tilt in India's official position in the international negotiations is clear from a proposal moved by India for the development of industry standards for 'special dietary foods' as a means to treat malnutrition. According to the proposal, specific standards should be developed for 'enhancing the cereal content, minimum protein contents and energy density' of packaged food 'for preventing and addressing the nutritional needs of underweight infants and young children.'[78] Independent observers see the Indian proposal as an industry move to bring in a 'market-based intervention' to address malnutrition.

The writing on the wall – or should we say the belly – is clear. Indian diets are getting globalized, increasing the prevalence of obesity and thereby the risk of heart disease. A complex state-industry nexus is responsible for the changing food environment in favour of unhealthy foods.

Barriers to Physical Activity

> 'The levels of energy expenditure as people go about their lives continue to shrink. [Many] people ... simply shift from one chair to another – from the chair in the car to the chair in the office to the chair in front of the television.'
>
> – David Dunstan, Baker IDI Heart and Diabetes Institute, Australia

Just as changes in our food environment are silently contributing to the risk of heart disease, the changing physical environment too has a big role to play in pushing the heart disease epidemic in India. Physical inactivity is considered a major factor causing lifestyle diseases. However, it is important to emphasize that lack of physical activity poses a risk in addition to unhealthy diets. It is not physical inactivity alone which is to blame for the lifestyle diseases, as the food industry is desperately trying to project in a bid to deflect the blame it is facing.

'Physical activity' should not be confused with physical exercise. Exercise is a subcategory of physical activity and is a 'planned, structured, repetitive, and purposeful' activity aimed at the improvement or maintenance of one or more components of physical fitness. On the other hand, according to the WHO, physical activity includes 'exercise as well as other activities which involve bodily movement and are done as part of playing, working, active transportation, house chores and recreational activities.'

Regular physical activity decreases the risk of death due to cardiovascular diseases, particularly that posed by coronary heart disease (CHD). The benefit regular physical activity offers in terms of reducing the risk of death is similar to that one enjoys when one does not smoke. Exercise reduces blood pressure in people suffering from hypertension, while regular physical activity prevents or delays the development of high blood pressure. The link between obesity and heart disease is strong, although much of it is ascribed to an increase in blood pressure and cholesterol levels.[1]

The level of one's physical activity depends on the type of physical environment. This usually consists of urban and rural settings, modes of transport to commute to work and those used to drop children to schools, the facilities available for children to play and adults to undertake physical activity. The expansion of cities, growing urbanization, rural to urban migration, changing profiles of personal transport, and urban and town planning are the key elements that shape our physical environment.

Physical or built environment, which includes buildings, roads, footpaths etc., is defined by land use patterns, transportation systems and design features that together provide opportunities for travel and physical activity in urban areas. The opportunities people get to remain physically active depend on the type of built environment in an area or a city. For example, parks and gardens with ready access can encourage people to walk about and engage in some physical exercise. Well-designed walking paths and pedestrian walkways are important for people who want to make short 'utilitarian' trips to markets, offices and schools nearby. A built environment can either encourage or discourage such opportunities. For instance, if footpaths are too high or are occupied by stray dogs and

> 'Physical activity' should not be confused with physical exercise. Exercise is a subcategory of physical activity.

Regular physical activity reduces the risk of coronary heart disease, stroke, diabetes, colon cancer as well the risk of breast cancer in women.

cattle or are dirty or not well lit at night, they hinder physical activity.

A built environment is influenced by policies cutting across several agencies like town planning, traffic police, electricity utilities, public transport, municipality and so on and is governed by a plethora of laws and guidelines. Making changes in a built environment may be difficult because of economic constraints, but in a country like India, where new infrastructure is being built and the existing infrastructure is being renovated, there may be opportunities to remove the barriers standing in the way of physical activity. Existing structures can be retrofitted in ways that make them conducive to physical activity. A built environment is often seen as a key reason for reduced levels of physical activity in Indian cities.

A built environment that promotes physical activity is important for heart health, because physical inactivity has been recognized as an independent risk factor for coronary heart disease and is considered a global health problem. The WHO defines physical activity as 'any bodily movement produced by skeletal muscles that requires energy expenditure.' At least thirty minutes of regular, moderate-intensity physical activity is considered essential to maintain the energy balance of the human body and control weight. Regular physical activity reduces the risk of coronary heart disease, stroke, diabetes, colon cancer as well as the risk of breast cancer in women. Individuals should engage in adequate levels of physical activity throughout their lives.

Policies that Hinder Physical Activity

Exercise is an individual option while physical activity has societal dimensions. The level of physical activity one undertakes depends on the quality of the physical or built environment one lives in.

That's why we need policies and strategies that can be implemented at the population level to tackle physical inactivity and promote physical activity. But instead of adopting such, India is vigorously pursuing ones that are pushing us towards physical inactivity.

There is enough scientific evidence that physical inactivity by itself is a leading cause of chronic diseases. An estimated 1.9 million deaths globally are attributed to physical inactivity. At least 60 per cent of the world's population fails to follow the thirty-minute-a-day physical activity regime required to remain healthy. This is because of insufficient leisure-time activities involving physical exercise and an increase in sedentary behaviour during work and while at home. An increase in the use of 'passive' modes of transport has also been associated with a decline in physical activity levels.

Levels of inactivity are high in virtually all developed and developing countries. In developed countries, more than half of the adult population is not active enough. In rapidly growing cities of the developing world, physical inactivity poses an even greater problem. Urbanization has made way for environmental factors that may discourage participation in physical activity: population over-crowding, increased poverty, increased levels of crime, high-density traffic, poor air quality, absence of parks, sidewalks, sports and recreation facilities.

Physical inactivity begins at home. Like elsewhere in the world, labour-saving devices are making urban Indians lead more and more sedentary lifestyles. Most of the domestic work is done with the help of electrical or motorized appliances that require minimum physical effort. Washing machines, dishwashers, vacuum cleaners, mixers and grinders, microwave ovens etc., have made urban living comfortable. In high-income groups in India, the penetration of washing machines increased by 20 per

Physical inactivity begins at home. Like elsewhere in the world, labour-saving devices are making urban Indians lead more and more sedentary lifestyles.

cent between 1990 and '99. Most of urban India – rich as well as poor – has mixer-grinders at home. Overall, its penetration has increased by 16 per cent uniformly across all segments of society except the lowest income groups during the same period.[2] Nobody can say no to labour-saving devices or want to go back to a time when all such devices were unavailable. We can also not undermine the aspirations of people to acquire new devices as incomes rise. Since these devices have made our lives comfortable and sedentary, we need to undertake more physical activity in order to compensate for the physical energy we save by using such devices.

The number of hours we spend in not undertaking any physical activity is rising. At home, people of all age groups spend more time in front of the television, computer screens or with gaming consoles, smart phones and tablets. The amount of 'screen time' has a direct bearing on the time children spend outdoors for cycling or playing games. A small study involving 350 persons suffering from acute myocardial infarction and 700 healthy individuals of similar backgrounds in Delhi and Bangalore revealed a direct relationship between physical inactivity and the occurrence of heart disease.[3] Those admitted to hospitals with heart disease reported that they had spent more time on sedentary activities, such as watching television, listening to music, reading and writing. Much of the sedentary time – an average 3.6 hours – was spent on watching television. Scientists who conducted the study pointed out that physical inactivity levels among urban Indians had reached the same levels as in the West.

The link between television viewing and a higher risk of heart disease observed in the Indian study was further highlighted by Australian researchers, who found that each hour spent in front of the television daily increased the risk of cardiovascular disease (CVD) related deaths by 18 per cent.[4] This was after making adjustments for other risk factors like smoking, high blood pressure and unhealthy diet. 'Social and economic changes mean that people don't move their muscles as much as they used to. Consequently, the levels of energy expenditure as people go about their lives continue to shrink. For many people on a daily basis it is simply shifting from one chair to another – from the chair in the car to the chair in the office to the chair in front of the television,' said David Dunstan, who led the study.[5]

Once out of their homes, people use passive modes of transport, which require minimum physical activity. Children go to school either in hired taxis, buses or use personal transport. Just a handful cycle or walk to school either because the roads are not considered safe enough for them to cycle or the distances involved are too long. An increasing number of adults use passive modes of transport – motorcycles, scooters or cars – to commute to work instead of active modes of transport like buses and local trains. The number of people who walk or cycle to work in Indian cities is a tiny minority. In the workplace too, more and more people are working in multistorey buildings where they use elevators to reach their offices and then work in front of computers. The growth of the service industry is unwittingly contributing a great deal to sedentary lifestyles.

Unlike the West, where people go fishing or biking during weekends, activities during the leisure time in case of the Indian urban middle class involves going to shopping malls in cars, watching a movie or eating out. Malls, which provide air-conditioned and pollution-free environments, have become the new symbols of urbanism. Recreational activities such as going to a park or watching a game are increasingly becoming rare these days. In rural areas too, the levels of physical activity seem to be going down. Dr Naresh Trehan, a leading cardiac surgeon said, 'Farmers used to be out in the field working. Now they are on tractors. The urban population, they are driving in cars everywhere. If they

Once out of their homes, people use passive modes of transport, which require minimum physical activity. Children go to school either in hired taxis, buses or use personal transport.

could drive to the bathroom, they would. We have become lazy.'[6] We are not questioning why more and more farms are becoming mechanized, we are underlining the need for physical activity even in rural areas.

Physical inactivity is not necessarily the cause of obesity. Obesity is a result of an energy imbalance. People gain weight when their total energy intake exceeds the total energy expenditure over a long period of time. On the other hand, physical activity relates to expenditure, which helps one to maintain a healthy balance between energy intake and expenditure. Physical inactivity – which may be prevalent among a larger section of people as compared to obesity – promotes sedentary behaviour and is an independent public health problem.

The National Family Health Survey conducted in 2005–06 gave some insights about obesity in India.[7] Although the percentage of women and men who are overweight or obese in India is not nearly as high as it is in many developed countries, the survey showed it is an emerging problem, especially in urban Indians, among those with higher education levels and those living in high-income households.

Recently, there has been an increase in the number of people migrating from villages to cities and towns. The reason for this is the Indian economy's gradual transformation into a service economy from a predominently agrarian one. Rural and semi-rural areas are also getting urbanized at the same time. The rate of urban growth in India is very high compared to developed countries. The 2011 census showed that the population of urban residents was 31.16 per cent of the total population.[8] Not just this, for the first time since Independence, the rise in urban population was higher than that of rural population in a decade. In some states like Tamil Nadu, the proportion of urban to total population has become nearly half.

While the expansion of urban areas and cities is definitely an indicator of the country's economic growth, the burden of non-communicable diseases resulting from this process has gone virtually unnoticed. The process of urbanization – migration from villages to cities and the expansion of urban areas into the periphery – is linked to changes in diet and behaviour. Rural migrants live in unhealthy conditions in slums. They are unable to support their traditional eating habits in city environs and largely depend on cheap but unhealthy food stuff available near the slums.

Several studies have reported the direct health impact of urbanization. For instance, one study conducted by the All India Institute of Medical Sciences (AIIMS), New Delhi, in 2008, concluded that living in urban areas increases the risk of hypertension. Migration to urban areas causes high blood pressure, which can lead to heart disease. In Orissa, a significantly higher prevalence of hypertension was reported in a tribal population living in a city compared to people of the same tribe living in villages.[9] A large study undertaken among rural migrants working in four cities – Lucknow, Nagpur, Hyderabad and Bangalore – showed that rural-urban migration in India is associated with the rapid increase in obesity and diabetes and also indicated that changes in migrant behaviour – such as reduced physical activity – put them at a similar risk as the urban population.[10]

The phenomenon of growing urbanization and expansion of cities has presented new challenges to the transport sector. Bigger cities mean increased travel demand as people have to travel longer distances for work, business and social appointments. In urban India, 75 per cent of the road trips are made to go to the workplace and transporting children to schools. When incomes rise, the number of 'discretionary' trips that people make grows – trips made for shopping, social activities and what can be categorized as 'personal business'. This trend has been seen in mega cities across the world, but all of them don't have the same level

The process of urbanization – migration from villages to cities and the expansion of urban areas into the periphery – is linked to changes in diet and behaviour.

of road congestion as in Delhi or Bangalore. This is because the mode of transport chosen to accomplish these trips determines the level of congestion on the roads. And it is very much a function of policy. In most cities of the world, a majority of distances to be covered is less than 10 km while most distances are less than 5 km in India.

With the change in the physical environment of Indian cities, the share of trips made by cycling and walking, both of which involve physical activity, is going down. The share of cycling in various modes of transport in Indian cities has declined from 30 per cent in 1994 to 11 per cent in 2008 due to factors like traffic congestion, increase in distances due to the urban sprawl, increase in the purchasing power of people and inadequate facilities for cycling. This was revealed in a study involving thirty cities sponsored by the Indian government in 2008.[11] The percentage of roads with pedestrian footpaths is hardly 30 in most cities that were surveyed. This means that people are forced to walk on roads, which makes them much more vulnerable to accidents. Nearly 40 per cent of trips in Indian cities are by non-motorized transport and 25 per cent of all fatal accidents involve cyclists and pedestrians.

About 30 per cent of all road trips in India are on foot, but this figure tends to drop as cities expand. The study also measured the walkability index of Indian cities. The national average index was 0.52. The best in the country according to this ranking is Chandigarh with 0.9 points. This is in sharp contrast to cities like London that score between 1.5 and 1.7 and have active policies to encourage pedestrian traffic. A low rank indicates inadequate and substandard pedestrian facilities. Delhi, Mumbai and Kolkata have a walkability index that is above the national average.

In addition, the share of public transport is constantly dipping – 60 per cent of all motorized trips in Delhi in the beginning of 2000 to 43 per cent in 2008. The share is expected to drop further in future in both small and big cities of India. An overall drop from 26 per cent in 2007 to 17 per cent in 2021 and 14 per cent in 2031 is expected. In mega cities where the share is higher, it is expected to drop to 36 per cent. Any attempt to augment public transport and increase its usage will lead to a corresponding increase in walking as it has been estimated that public transport users also walk four times every day.

A large number of people generally walk to have access to essential services like education, local shoppping, leisure trips in the neighbourhood and jobs since many of these trips usually require them to cover distances of less than 2 km. But, increasingly, walking trips within this range are being replaced by motorized trips due to hostile walking conditions, according to a 2009 study.[12] All the residential colonies that were surveyed scored poorly on the walkability index. Overall, the study said, 'car-centric infrastructure for seamless, signal-free travel through flyovers, expressways and elevated ways, is severing the urban landscape, disrupting the direct shortest routes of the walkers and increasing the distances and travel time for them.'

The insatiable need for space for motorized vehicles is leading to an arbitrary surrender of walking spaces in cities, transport experts feel. In most places, the survey found, walking spaces are being given up to make way for cars to park. Changes made in a city's built environment through road–engineering interventions could permanently decide the design of the network and influence the travel choices of people, experts feel. The construction of multi-level flyovers with loops – for the Commonwealth Games 2010 – at major intersections in Delhi ignored the needs of pedestrians and non-motorized transport such as cycles and rickshaws. There are lesser traffic lights to facilitate almost signal-free rides for motorists, but few footbridges for pedestrians who risk their lives while crossing roads; cyclists have to take detours which are longer and discouraging. No steps have been taken to ensure that the road design does not increase

> The bias towards motorized traffic is making civic agencies surrender walking spaces arbitrarily.

dependence on and the usage of personal motorized vehicles. This will be possible only if the policy focus shifts to public transport, walking and cycling.

The share of personal transport like a car or a two-wheeler increases simultaneously, resulting in chaos on the roads and very low average speed. Faulty urban transport and other policies are to blame for the tilt in favour of personal, motorized modes of transport at the cost of non-motorized modes prevalent earlier. Public policies also do not promote the public transport system in the manner it deserves. As per official data, while the population of India's six major metropolises increased by about 1.9 times between 1981 and 2001, the number of motor vehicles went up by over 7.75 times during the same period.

Let's see how public policies favoured the growth of the automobile industry.

The 'small car revolution' in India is a result of a government initiative. In 1982, Maruti Udyog Limited was set up as a state-owned company in collaboration with Japan's Suzuki to produce a small mass-market car. More options became available when the economy opened up in the early 1990s. The automobile sector was delicensed, and this helped all leading car companies to set up their factories in India. The government's auto policy looks at this industry as a revenue earner as it accounts for 17 per cent of the indirect tax revenue. The main objective of the auto policy, formulated by the Ministry of Heavy Industries, is 'to promote integrated, phased, enduring and self-sustained growth of the Indian automotive industry'.[13] Keeping the thrust on volume production in mind, the policy advocates fiscal incentives for greater indigenous capability for small cars. The low ownership of cars in India – 6 per thousand as against 500 in developed economies – is cited to justify the thrust towards the increasing demand for cars.

The government thinks personal cars are a substitute for public transport. The policy recognizes multi-utility vehicles as 'an important mode of economical mass transport in rural India' because the road infrastructure in rural areas is poor and a 'good state transport system' is lacking. Since these vehicles 'are the first ones to be purchased by a number of farmers, traders and small businessmen in rural and semi-urban markets, the government will endeavour to provide fiscal incentives to this sector.' Remember, most of these multi-utility vehicles run on diesel. So the state provides double incentives to promote diesel cars – fiscal incentives as envisaged in the auto policy and incentives in the form of diesel subsidy.

To fulfil these policy objectives, a number of fiscal measures are followed. The import of capital goods and automotive components were placed under OGL. There was promotion of R&D in the automotive industry with the help of fiscal and financial incentives. It also encouraged the setting up of independent automotive design firms by providing tax breaks, concessional duty on plant, equipment imports and granting automatic approvals.

State governments offered cheap land, free electricity, water and tax holidays in order to attract investment from automobile companies.

The car industry gets government help in several other forms, as environment activist Sunita Narain elaborated in 2008: 'There is the cost of regulating traffic; of installing traffic signals; of building flyovers, over-bridges and subways; of pollution control measures; of the health problems we face after breathing in the fumes being emitted from the vehicles. Since cars take up over 75 per cent of road space, even though they transport less than 20 per cent of the people, it is obvious whom this expenditure benefits the most.'[14] There is also the cost of congestion – the average driving speed in Delhi during peak hours came down from almost 30 km per hour in 1997 to around 10 km per hour in 2006.

The policy recognizes multi-utility vehicles as 'an important mode of economical mass transport in rural India' because the road infrastructure in rural areas is poor and a 'good state transport system' is lacking.

In addition, car owner pays a one-time road tax, which is between 0.5–5 per cent of the cost of the vehicle in most states. But bus owners have to pay an annual road tax and also a passenger tax based on the number of people a bus carries. A lifetime road tax on passenger cars ranges from Rs 2925 in Manipur to Rs 40,000 in Tamil Nadu. A car in Delhi, if amortized for useful life, attracts only Rs 300 a year as road tax, while a bus owner is charged over Rs 13,000 – about forty-three times more. In Mumbai, buses attract a road tax of Rs 41,000 a year, but cars pay a lifetime tax of only Rs 9000. Buses are taxed on the basis of their seating capacity, the distance they cover in a day and the type of routes they ply on. The annual road tax on buses is as high as Rs 60,000 in Kerala and Rs 50,000 in Karnataka. In effect, buses have to pay a penalty for efficiency as they move more people, take up less road space, consume less fuel and emit less carbon per passenger.

As the auto policy envisages increasing car production and per capita usage, it also argues in favour of the creation of parking facilities. Starting with metropolitan and important towns, it says, the government will pursue amendments to bye-laws with state governments and local bodies for 'upward revision of the parking norms for new residential buildings, construction of common parking for existing residential areas besides parking upgradation in all commercial areas'. Multistorey parking shall also be encouraged.[15]

Egged on by the economic boom, the auto industry and the government promoting it are going that extra mile to increase car ownership in India. Transport experts are worried that increasing car ownership will only add to the urban chaos. The basic problem is not the number of vehicles in the country but their concentration in a few selected cities, particularly metropolises. It is alarming to note that 32 per cent of all vehicles are plying in metropolitan cities alone; these cities constitute about 11 per cent of country's total urban population.[16]

While the auto policy and subsequent steps to implement it encourage greater use of motor cars and sports utility vehicles, the

The basic problem is not the number of vehicles in the country but their concentration in a few selected cities, particularly in metropolises.

National Urban Transport Policy (NUTP) adopted in April 2006 blamed 'an explosive growth in the number of motor vehicles, coupled with limitations on the amount of road space' for the congestion on roads and seeks to 'encourage greater use of public transport and non-motorized modes by offering central financial assistance'.[17]

Clearly, two wings of the same government are trying to promote policies which are at loggerheads. One of the key objectives of the transport policy is to bring about 'a more equitable allocation of road space with people, rather than focusing on the vehicles.' Since road space gets allocated to whichever vehicle occupies it first, the focus is the vehicle and not the people. As a result, a bus carrying forty people is allocated only two and a half times the road space allocated to a car carrying only one or two persons. So users of a bus, which is an 'active' mode of transport from the health point of view, end up with higher travel time and travel costs, compared to the disproportionate space allocated to personal vehicles, which are a 'passive' mode of transport. Pedestrians, cyclists and other non-motorized modes of transport – all healthy and cheaper options – have been elbowed out. Also, users of these modes are at a higher risk of being run over.

In order to shift the focus from vehicles to people and to allocate road space on a more equitable basis, the policy says the central government would encourage reserving lanes and corridors exclusively for public transport and non-motorized modes of travel. At best, this is a noble idea which remains on paper. Forget separate lanes, local administrations in Delhi, Gurgaon and Noida have imposed restrictions on the number of cycle rickshaws and their movement. The Lieutenant Governor of Delhi ordered the demolition of newly constructed pavements and cycle tracks in May 2010, as 'they are eating into road space'.[18] The cap on the number of rickshaws imposed by the Municipal Corporation of Delhi had to be struck down by the Delhi High Court in February 2010. The court noted that Delhi roads were clogged because it had some 6 million motorized vehicles of which 4 million were cars and sports utility vehicles, which served the transport needs of just 20 per cent of people, and observed that 'road space cannot be appropriated or monopolized by one mode of transport, particularly when the bulk of the population depends on public transport'.

The auto policy advocates creation of more parking facilities for cars in residential as well as commercial areas and suggests multistorey parking lots, but the NUPT says that parking lots occupy large tracts of land and therefore a higher parking fee that reflects the value of the land occupied should be levied. A high parking fee, it says, should be used as a means to make the use of public transport more attractive. While allocating parking space, preference should be given to public transport vehicles and non-motorized modes of transport. Once again, there seems to be no takers for this government policy. In fact, the government itself appears to lack the will to implement its own policy. Footpaths have been levelled off in most places in Delhi, including in residential colonies, so that they can double up as free parking lots.

Instead of improving road quality and public transport infrastructure – the lack of which are cited as a justification for state policies favouring personal transport – the policy thrust is on building multistorey parking lots for cars. An automated parking lot near the Delhi High Court cost the government Rs 182 crore and it has parking space for 1450 cars. This means the government has spent nearly Rs 1 crore towards the parking of eight private vehicles. The Environment Pollution (Prevention & Control) Authority (EPCA) for the National Capital Region noted in 2006 that 'the provision of parking for personal motorized vehicles cannot be considered a matter of public good. The individual user of a personal vehicle should pay for the use of the parking space.'

> Instead of improving road quality and public transport infrastructure, the policy thrust is on building multistorey parking for cars.

Parking facilities – underground, surface and multilevel – are provided at an enormous cost. They end up using a lot of public money and cheap or free land. According to an estimate provided to the authority by the New Delhi Municipal Council (NDMC), the real cost of parking a car in Delhi would be Rs 100 per hour if just the capital cost of providing multilevel parking is factored in. The rate of car parking in the city is Rs 10. This means the government is providing a subsidy of Rs 90 for every car parked in public parking lots. 'If public agencies are responsible for funding these (parking) structures or providing land as part of their share in a public-private partnership, this will amount to subsidy for the rich car users. This is against the principle of equity. Therefore, the 'user pays' principle should govern the pricing of parking,' the EPCA felt.[19] The authority suggested that the demand for parking should be managed through a well-thought-out pricing policy.

Government agencies are constructing multilevel parking lots in all major Indian cities either by themselves or in partnership with private builders, as suggested in the government's auto policy. These complexes are very expensive to build. The cost of one equivalent car space (ECS) parking in a manual multilevel parking area is Rs 3 lakh, whereas in a mechanized parking lot it would be Rs 6 lakh per ECS. The operation and maintenance cost of the multilevel parking complex is very high and it is difficult to recover the cost of the project from the revenue earned from parking. Given all this, such new structures find few takers. In order to make the venture attractive and viable for private builders, the government is allowing them to earn through other commercial activities in multilevel parking structures. This changes the land use of the designated parking area and encourages private profits, according to the EPCA.

On-street parking – a major cause of congestion on Indian roads – continues to be free in most thoroughfares in Indian cities.

This, coupled with the poor enforcement of no-parking regulations, undermines the occupancy and viability of multilevel parking facilities.[20] The logic behind free on-street parking is the one-time tax collected by local bodies at the time of purchase of a new car. This amount is too low – in Delhi it is between Rs 3000 to Rs 5000 per car, compared to what the government spends on parking facilities. In 2011, twenty-seven multilevel parking structures were under construction for a total cost of several billion rupees.

The availability of land to construct parking complexes is another problem. About 10 per cent of land in Delhi is used for parking. The parking space required in any city does not just depend on the number of vehicles. Every car needs three parking spaces – at the owner's home, at his or her workplace and at any place one goes to shop or for entertainment. To overcome the shortage of prime land for parking, the Municipal Corporation of Delhi (MCD) proposed the construction of underground parking areas beneath parks and playgrounds in the city. It sought permission from the EPCA after it began work on nine such parking complexes. The authority in February 2010 'reluctantly conceded that the MCD could proceed only in respect of the nine sites' with the conditions that after construction, 90 per cent of the site area would be transformed into playgrounds and landscaping would be done using shrubs and grass. Trees would be planted on the remaining 10 per cent of the land on the sides and a small portion would be used as a ramp.

Though Delhi still boasts open spaces and neighbourhood parks in residential areas, such green spaces are constantly under threat. Children wanting to play in these parks are often at loggerheads with elders representing residents' associations. One of them petitioned in the Delhi High Court against children using a colony park to play football. Rejecting the petition, the court remarked, 'If children are not permitted to play in parks too, they will be left with no other place except the busy streets to play on, severely affecting their behavioural pattern, growth and health. The same holds true for grown-ups wanting to indulge in some physical activity either before or after work.'[21] This is not an isolated case, many such resident associations are trying to convert open spaces in their colonies into 'ornamental parks' in collaboration with the MCD under a public-private partnership, leaving little space for children to play.

There is an increase in the number of vehicles running on diesel because of the diesel subsidy. This is quite worrisome since it leads to congestion on the roads and gives rise to health problems. Cars are the second largest users of diesel in the country, guzzling more volume than the agriculture sector and buses.

Globally, several studies have connected heart disease with exposure to traffic, air pollution (particularly diesel fumes) and congestion on roads. A research paper published in the 26 August 2008 issue of the *Journal of the American College of Cardiology* identified short- and long-term toxic effects of air pollution, which it said can cause injury to heart and blood vessels, increase the rates of hospitalization for treatment of cardiac ailments and even result in death. When inhaled, pollutants boost 'superoxiding' molecules that damage the cells, cause inflammation of the lungs and have a harmful effect on the cardiovascular system. In addition, ultrafine pollutants – like the ones being emitted from an automobile exhaust – can enter the blood stream and directly damage the heart and blood vessels. Such fine particles are capable of leading to an immediate drop in both coronary blood flow and affect the heart's pumping function.

In September 2008, researchers wrote in the medical journal *Circulation* that microscopic air pollutants can adversely affect the heart's ability to conduct electrical signals in people with serious coronary artery disease. British and Swedish researchers in their papers presented at the American Heart Association's Scientific sessions in November 2007

> When inhaled, pollutants boost 'superoxiding' molecules that damage cells, cause inflammation of the lungs, and damage the cardiovascular system.

reported that diesel exhaust amplifies clot formation and blood platelet activity in healthy volunteers, which could lead to heart attack and stroke. Blood is more likely to clot when a person is exposed to relatively high levels of diesel exhaust for a short time. The clot could lead to a blocked vessel resulting in heart attack or stroke. Diesel exhaust is particularly harmful for the heart. It has been linked to atherosclerosis or hardening of the arteries, which significantly increases the risk of heart attack and stroke.

Scientists from the University of California in Los Angeles, in their study results published in the 26 July 2007 edition of the online journal *Genome Biology*, explained how fine particles in air pollution join with artery-clogging fats to switch on genes that cause blood vessel inflammation and lead to cardiovascular disease. Unmindful of the grave health risks of using diesel, diesel-powered automobiles are gaining popularity in India because of the increased fuel economy and the boost provided by government policies.

Policy Vacuum on Physical Activity

There are government policies in various sectors that directly or indirectly promote physical inactivity, but when it comes to promoting physical activity and wellness there is nothing. We have seen how state policies encourage the use of motorized forms of personal transport and discourage the use of public transport and non-motorized modes such as cycles. We have also seen ways in which the state promotes the use of unhealthy food and influences the dietary habits of people. These factors, along with inadequate promotion of physical activity and health education, result in high physical inactivity levels.

> The role of schools is very critical because regular physical activity is not only necessary for the overall growth and development of children, it also prevents early onset of non-communicable diseases.

Government departments and ministries need to initiate policies and action to address the issue of physical inactivity as they address other risk factors of heart disease. It should begin with the health ministry. India does not have uniform, scientifically designed physical activity guidelines for its citizens. The National Institute of Nutrition defines that 'a minimum 30–45 minutes of brisk walk/ physical activity of moderate intensity improves the overall health', as part of its dietary guidance. But no comprehensive guidelines on physical activity exist. In the absence of such guidelines, there are a few private initiatives that define the level of physical activity Indians need to undertake in order to remain healthy. We need to encourage physical activity at home, schools, workplace and even at the community level.

The role of schools is very critical because regular physical activity is not only necessary for the overall growth and development of children, it also prevents the early onset of non-communicable diseases and makes people aware about fitness. Health and fitness policies exist at the school level but mostly remain ineffective. The Central Board of Secondary Education (CBSE) has directed all schools affiliated to the board to include performance of students in games and sports in the continuous and comprehensive evaluation (CCE) scheme. It has stipulated that every day there should be at least one forty-minute period dedicated to physical activity and games for all sections from classes 1 to 10. For classes 11 and 12, at least two periods per week should be devoted to physical activity, games or yoga. But schools are reluctant to implement this order. Many of them face constraints of space, while others feel that it would cut into academic time.

Yoga keeps one's body and mind healthy. It represents the classical Indian system of physical exercise but it was somehow lost over the years. Yoga was restricted to practitioners and ashrams run by yogis and sages. In recent decades, however, yoga has been rediscovered thanks to the attention it is attracting in the West. Yoga presents an option not only for the preservation and

Every educational institution should have adequate facilities for recreation, adventure and sports activities, including playgrounds.

promotion of health, but also for better disease management. Yogic interventions have been prescribed and researched for the management of stress-induced and psychosomatic disorders, as well as for heart disease. The Morarji Desai National Institute of Yoga in Delhi, run by the Ministry of Health, launched a scheme to fund private bodies in yoga training and education.

The National Youth Policy, announced in 2003, has a section on promoting physical activity but the Ministry of Youth Affairs and Sports which formulated it does not have any programme to implement the same. The policy enunciates that 'sports and games be promoted as a mass movement by making them a way of life' and recommends making 'sports, games and physical education including yoga' compulsory in all educational institutions.[22] The policy says that every educational institution should have adequate facilities for recreation, adventure and sports activities, including playgrounds. Provisions should be made for common playgrounds in master plans of all civic and municipal areas. Rural, traditional and indigenous sports would be accorded special attention and it would be the responsibility of panchayat institutions with the help of local youth organizations to develop and maintain the infrastructure for this.

Conclusions

We have ample evidence about the state subsidizing the use of personal motorized transport in different ways, at the cost of public transport systems and individual use of non-motorized modes of transport, which are not only economical and sustainable but also healthy for people's hearts. This has a direct bearing on the heart disease epidemic in India because physical inactivity has been recognized as a key determinant in the development of coronary artery disease. How can we expect people to walk, cycle, hop on to a public bus or a rickshaw when there are no pedestrian paths, parks or cycling tracks, or when public transport is unsafe and inefficient?

The current urban physical infrastructure will give rise to higher levels of physical inactivity and thus obesity and associated health problems. This is what has been seen in America, where a superb highway system and the supreme position held by the auto industry has made car travel a dominant way of transport in the past six decades. Researchers at the University of Illinois have found a link between driving and surging levels of obesity in the US.[23] Promotion of cycling and walking, coupled with fewer cars, can save the lives of over 14,000 people every year in Delhi as reported in a study published in *The Lancet* in November 2009.[24] In Delhi alone, there would be an 11 to 25 per cent decrease in the total heart disease burden, which means preventing around 2490 to 7140 premature deaths every year. Similarly, up to 3650 stroke deaths and 460 deaths on account of diabetes could also be prevented. In addition, almost 3000 deaths due to traffic accidents could be prevented. Active travel should become the mode of choice instead of just being the mode of necessity for those unable to afford cars. The notion that if someone is cycling he or she cannot afford a car and vice versa should be done away with.

All city development blueprints should include an explicit pedestrian plan. A comprehensive law on road use should be enacted to ensure the segregation of space by users and a system of penalty should be imposed to prevent encroachment in pedestrian space and to prevent its gobbling up for motorized traffic without proper justification. All this is necessary to make people feel safe and secure on walkways and cross walks. Currently, pedestrians account for the largest number of road deaths in Indian cities. Nearly 80,000 die, 1.2 million are seriously injured and about 300,000 are disabled permanently every year. City plans should also include community sports facilities, swimming pools, recreation centres and well-maintained public parks with walking paths, benches for the elderly, toilets etc.

Along with the creation of a favourable physical environment for cycling and walking, the government should also invest in a robust public transport system. In 2009, the Ministry of Urban Development announced a massive one-time grant of over Rs 4720 crore to states for the purchase of 15,000 buses to be deployed in fifty-nine cities. The grant was linked to conditional reforms in the transport sector such as higher taxes on private cars, dedicated funds for public transport and use of parking policy to discourage car use. However, the reforms did not include promotion of walking and cycling. The pedestrian infrastructure should be planned to cater to the present and future demand for walking that will be generated from a higher usage of public transport.

Thus heart disease is not just a health issue but is closely linked to policies in a number of other sectors: urban development, city planning, public transport, fuel subsidies, automobile, urban renewal and so on. Unless corrective measures are taken to make all these policies heart-friendly, any effort made in the health sector to tackle lifestyle diseases would remain subcritical.

The Poison Leaf

> 'Tobacco industry in India contributes in a unique manner to several important facets of the Indian economy, covering revenue, export, employment and GDP growth ... The growth of the cigarette industry represents a big revenue opportunity for the economy.'
>
> – Directorate of Tobacco, Government of India*

The tobacco industry occupies a special place in the policy apparatus of the Indian government. A commodity which is a foremost killer in the eyes of medical experts is given pride of place by different departments of the Indian government. Some government agencies are engaged in actively promoting this industry, even going as far as to bestow it with annual awards for 'best' performance every year.

The consumption of tobacco – one of the most important predisposing factors for heart disease in India – is widespread. About 10 per cent of the world's tobacco users are in India, a country which is the world's third largest producer of tobacco leaves. Every year Indians smoke about 107 billion cigarettes and anywhere between 750 billion and 1.2 trillion bidis. In 2004, a study

* 'Role in economy', Directorate of Tobacco Development, Ministry of Agriculture, website: http://dtd.dacnet.nic.in/, accessed 15 March 2013.

commissioned by the Ministry of Health estimated the number of tobacco users (smokers and chewers) aged ten years and above to be 250 million. Another large study published by the Centre for Global Health Research at the University of Toronto in 2008 put the figure of smokers alone at over 120 million Indians.[1] Tobacco use is prevalent in 43 per cent males and 7 per cent females in urban areas, according to the data collected by the National Sample Survey Organisation (NSSO). In rural areas, these figures are 64.4 per cent among males and 15.5 per cent among females. The overall prevalence rate of tobacco use in the country was pegged at 35.5 per cent. There is proof that smoking and usage of chewable tobacco is prevalent among school-going boys and girls in cities and villages. Two in every ten boys and one in every ten girls use more than one tobacco product.

India accounts for one of the highest numbers of tobacco-related deaths in the world. Of 5.5 million people who die every year due to tobacco-related diseases globally, one million are in India. Smoking alone causes 700,000 deaths annually in the country. The leading cause of death due to tobacco has been found to be cardiovascular diseases, followed by chronic obstructive pulmonary disease and lung cancer. This makes heart disease the number one killer for tobacco users. The level of risk of a smoker suffering from coronary heart disease is 2.87 times more than that of a non-smoker. Tobacco use leads to almost 20 per cent of India's cardiovascular deaths.[2] It has, in fact, emerged as the major cause for the occurrence of premature cardiovascular diseases in India. This partly explains the high prevalence of heart disease and stroke among the poor, as tobacco consumption among them is very high.

There is proof that smoking and use of chewable tobacco is prevalent among school-going boys and girls in cities and villages. Two in every ten boys and one in every ten girls use more than one tobacco product.

The health consequences of tobacco are manifold. The most popular perception about smoking is that it causes lung cancer. But there are several other adverse effects too. Again, chewable tobacco is most often linked with mouth cancer. The fact is, it can cause several other diseases. Both smoking and smokeless tobacco (of the chewable variety) are particularly bad for the human heart. Nicotine raises the heart rate, blood pressure and blood fat. It causes the arteries to constrict, reducing blood supply to the heart. Other chemicals in tobacco smoke damage the innermost lining of the arteries, leading to their hardening and clogging. In addition, tobacco smokers ingest highly toxic carbon monoxide, which combines with haemoglobin in the blood and reduces its oxygen-carrying capacity. Smoking decreases exercise tolerance and increases the tendency for the blood to clot.

If one smokes tobacco, the risk of heart disease automatically increases. The risk increases manifold in the presence of other factors such as unhealthy diet and physical inactivity. Smoking also enhances the chances of the recurrence of heart disease in those who have undergone bypass surgery. Similarly, the use of smokeless tobacco can lead to high blood pressure, narrowing of the arteries of the heart and clotting of the blood, eventually leading to heart attacks.

Tobacco consumption in India has a long history and its story is interwoven into the cultural and social customs. Like tea, coffee and spices, tobacco too is closely linked with the fabled spice route that connected India with the Middle East, Europe and the West.[3] Portuguese sailors discovered the tobacco plant, which was treasured by the American-Indians for its presumed medicinal and obvious stimulant properties, and introduced it in Europe in the late fifteenth century. When they landed in India, they brought it with them. It was initially just a gift for the royals but gradually spread to the commoners as well. Tobacco was a favoured commodity

If one smokes tobacco, the risk of heart disease automatically increases. Smoking also enhances the chances of recurrence of heart diseases in those who have undergone bypass surgery.

in the barter trade between Europeans and Indians. When the British came they imported American tobacco into India and, later, the East India Company started growing it locally. Tobacco leaves grown in the Indian subcontinent were exported to Britain and cigarettes were imported back. As local consumption grew to a sizeable level, the Imperial Tobacco Company (ITC) began manufacturing cigarettes in colonial India.

Historically, bidi has always been a popular product used by the poor. This makes tobacco consumption patterns in India vastly different from those in the West. Bidi manufacturing started in the late nineteenth century. It was an indigenous innovation, a sort of portable alternative to hookah, which was tedious to carry and could be shared only among people of the same caste or clan. Labourers working in tobacco farms in Gujarat would roll leftover tobacco in dried leaves and smoke. Locally available leaves, mostly those from the astra, mango and sal trees, were used. When a couple of enterprising Gujarati businessmen visited Jabalpur in Madhya Pradesh, they found that tendu leaves abundantly available in the degraded forests there could be suitable for rolling bidis. Tendu leaves turned out to be excellent wrapping material; the dried leaves did not crack when rolled, they had a leathery texture and went well with the flavour of tobacco.[4] The first Indian bidi company was established in 1897, and, by 1930, several units came up all over the country.

Besides bidi and cigarette smoking, tobacco is consumed in a variety of forms in different parts of the country: chewing, applying, gargling and sucking. The use of dry tobacco products such as gutka, mawa and khaini is widespread and these products are highly addictive. Many of these products like khaini, which were packaged in backyard sheds and sold locally

Pan masala and gutka, a preparation of powdered tobacco, arecanut, lime, catechu and condiments, are other chewable products that spawned a multi-billion rupee industry in the past three decades.

in some regions, have now become commercially manufactured products widely marketed and advertised across the country. Pan masala and gutka, a preparation of powdered tobacco, arecanut, lime, catechu and condiments are other chewable products that spawned a multi-billion rupee industry in the past three decades. They are emerging as a major health threat.

Given its widespread use and serious health consequences, one would expect the Indian government to implement policies which discourage consumption of tobacco. But the Indian State is doing exactly the opposite.

State Support

Tobacco is a unique commodity. It is an agricultural crop but not a food item. It is grown by farmers like other agriculture crops but its benefits mainly flow to the industry. Tobacco is not a food item, yet it is consumed (smoked or chewed) by humans. It is sold for human consumption but is a major threat to human health. Government allows companies to manufacture and market tobacco products and at the same time issue health warnings. The tobacco industry takes full advantage of these apparent contradictions.

While the government recognizes the dangers tobacco poses to health, it continues to support it because it is an agriculture commodity and is supposed to be a major revenue earner. Its so-called benefit to the exchequer disappears if the health burden due to tobacco is taken into account. In order to silence the critics on this issue, the government ordered a study by the Indian Council of Medical Research. The study, a one-of-a-kind, estimated the cost due to three major tobacco-related diseases – cancers, heart disease and chronic lung disease – to the nation as Rs 27,760 crore in 1999.[5] The national cost due to heart disease attributed to tobacco was put at Rs 12,905 crore. In contrast, the total excise revenue on tobacco earned by the government for the same year, i.e., 1998–99, was a mere Rs 5500 crore.

Clearly, it is a misnomer that government support to the tobacco industry is justified because it is a major revenue earner. The health costs accrued by tobacco are several times higher than its revenue potential. Bidis and unfiltered cigarettes attract much lower taxes than filtered ones. Tax on handmade bidis, which constitute 98 per cent of total production, is nearly zero. Experts have recommended that higher taxation on all tobacco products will cut consumption rates while resulting in higher revenue for the government. Even a modest 10 per cent increase in bidi prices can reduce consumption by 9.2 per cent.[6]

The first time the state showed some health concern in relation to tobacco consumption was in 1975. By then, the link between tobacco and cancer as well as heart disease had been well established. Both international and Indian studies have shown an increased risk of heart disease in tobacco users. This was reflected in the preamble of India's first anti-tobacco law enacted in 1975, which stated that 'Smoking of cigarettes is a harmful habit and, in the course of time, can lead to grave health hazards. Research studies carried out in various parts of the world have confirmed that there is a relationship between smoking of cigarettes and lung cancer. Chronic bronchitis, certain diseases of the heart and the arteries, cancer of the bladder, prostrate, mouth, pharynx and oesophagus, peptic ulcer etc., are also reported to be among the ill effects of cigarette smoking.'

The Cigarettes (Regulation of Production, Supply and Distribution) Act, popularly known as the Cigarettes Act, 1975 – led to the introduction of statutory health warnings on cigarette packets. It was the first legislation related to health in which prevention of the disease was the main objective. However, the law had two major shortcomings – the warning

> Chronic bronchitis, certain diseases of the heart and the arteries, cancer of the bladder, prostrate, mouth, pharynx and oesophagus and peptic ulcer are some of the ill effects of cigarette smoking.

('Cigarette smoking is injurious to health') was too mild and it applied only to cigarettes and not to other major tobacco products (bidi, zarda, khaini or gutka). Despite these shortcomings, it remained the only tobacco control law for the next thirty years.

Ironically, the year in which the Cigarettes Act was passed, the Parliament also gave its approval to a pro-tobacco piece of legislation – The Tobacco Board Act of 1975 – to set up a dedicated state agency to promote tobacco trade in the country. While the Cigarettes Act was mooted by the Ministry of Health, the Ministry of Commerce was behind the Tobacco Board Act. Since India was then the third largest producer of tobacco in the world, the Ministry of Commerce felt the need for the central government to develop the tobacco industry and bring it under the control of the central government.

In fact, tobacco has occupied a prime place in the policy apparatus of the central government since 1947 when India gained independence. The Indian Central Tobacco Committee (ICTC) was set up in 1945 as the primary agency dealing with tobacco trade in the country. Then the Tobacco Export Promotion Council was set up to look after exports. The Tobacco Board took over all these responsibilities, and in addition, was put in charge of all related tasks such as research, crop development and trade in raw tobacco.

Three central government agencies currently promote tobacco trade, industry, research and consumption in the country. They are the Tobacco Board (Ministry of Commerce), Directorate of Tobacco Development (Department of Agriculture and Cooperation in the Ministry of Agriculture) and the Central Tobacco Research Institute (Department of Agriculture Research and Education, Ministry of Agriculture – CTRI). The last was set up by ICTC at Rajahmundry in Andhra Pradesh and was brought under the control of the Indian Council of Agriculture Research (ICAR) in 1965.

The mission of the tobacco board is 'to strive for the overall development of tobacco growers and the Indian tobacco industry.' One of its key functions is 'sponsoring, assisting, co-coordinating or encouraging scientific, technological and economic research for promotion of the tobacco industry.' The board declares on its website that it is 'committed to accomplishing its role – the expressed will of the Parliament – for the smooth functioning of a vibrant farming system, fair and remunerative prices to tobacco growers and export promotion'. But in effect, it is doing much more than just ensuring fair price to tobacco farmers and protecting their interests.

The Indian government virtually acts as an industry promotion body. The Tobacco Board is mandated to facilitate 'research, marketing, warehousing, publicity and promotion abroad, and extension of market intelligence in competing countries'. The board gives away awards to best cigarette manufacturers and exporters every year for producing more and more cigarettes, chewable tobacco and other tobacco products. In 2009, the Indian government bestowed the honour of 'Best Cigarette Manufacturer' in the country to ITC Limited. The second and third positions went to Godfrey Philips India Limited and VST Industries Limited respectively. In the chewable tobacco product category, the awards went to R.M. Dhaliwal, Kothari Products and Shree Meenakshi Food Products. Manufacturers of cut tobacco, hookah tobacco paste and snuff were also awarded. In all, thirty companies and thirty-six tobacco growers were awarded by the Indian government. In 2011 and 2012, ITC, Godfrey and VST were awarded for being the top three 'progressive cigarette traders'. ITC was also awarded for export of the cut variety of tobacco and cigarettes, along with manufacturers of chewable tobacco, gutka and hookah paste. ITC, Godfrey Phillips and VST were the top winners in 2013 as well. Dozens of tobacco farmers in several categories are also awarded every year. No food or fruit crop enjoys this kind of State patronage.

True to its name, the Directorate of Tobacco Development is yet another state instrument to promote tobacco in the country, though, functionally, its role overlaps with other agencies. It says 'Tobacco is a principal cash crop of national importance. It has been playing a prominent role in the development of the nation's economy.'[7]

> Government bodies like the Directorate of Tobacco Development are acting as tobacco promotion agencies and giving awards for higher cigarette production.

Although the cultivation of tobacco is restricted to 0.3 per cent of the total cultivated area, the body claims, tobacco provides employment to over 60 lakh Indians engaged in 'farming, curing, redrying, packaging, grading, manufacturing, distribution, export and retailing activities'. Bidi making, in its view, is the 'foremost cottage industry' in the country and 'the bidi industry derives some social significance from the fact that it generates more employment in the economy compared to the cigarette industry.' That's why the directorate sees 'scope for development of the bidi industry in view of excessive and biased tax treatment of cigarettes.'[8]

With government bodies like the directorate acting on behalf of the tobacco industry, it would seem the industry does not need to spend on advertising at all.

The directorate proudly declares, 'Although there is a nationwide anti-tobacco campaign, the commercial importance of tobacco can never be underestimated due to the revenue-earning potential and employment-generation capacity of the crop'. It also runs down efforts to substitute tobacco with other crops because 'research findings show that there is no economically viable alternative crop which is as remunerative as tobacco to the farmer. The difference in net returns from tobacco and the next best crop is significant'.[9] This difference, according to unsourced data posted on the website of the directorate, is Rs 4405 per hectare for farmers growing Bengal gram and Rs 875 for those growing chilli in Andhra Pradesh. To sum it up, the message from the government is clear: Farmers, please keep growing tobacco because it is a lucrative crop; it has no alternative.

The CTRI is engaged in research on every aspect of tobacco production – from soil and pest management to development of new and 'less harmful' varieties. 'The sustainability of Indian tobacco will depend more and more on making it less harmful,' the then secretary of the Department of Agriculture Research and Education, Mangala Rai, said in March 2007.[10] The institute, with a budget of Rs 112 crore in the Eleventh Five Year Plan, has an extensive research network spanning nineteen centres and stations working on tobacco suitable for different products like cigarette, bidi, cheroot, cigar, snuff and for chewing. The steady increase in tobacco consumption is a matter of satisfaction for this government-funded body. It said, 'Inspite of the anti-tobacco campaign gaining momentum, tobacco consumption the world over is increasing by 2 per cent and, hence, there is a need to produce quality tobacco with lower levels of harmful constituents and pesticide residues for export.'

Like the Tobacco Board and the Directorate, the CTRI too works closely with cigarette and bidi manufacturers. It set up a Tobacco Information Centre in 2003 'for the benefit of the tobacco fraternity'. It is working with ITC, Godfrey Phillips India and the Indian Tobacco Association (a lobby of tobacco biggies) on 'research and developmental activities, organization of training programmes, field trials on latest packages, variety release proposals, manufacturing of tests, storage tests, tobacco portal etc'. The CTRI even helps the industry to identify new market niches for Indian tobacco. The potential of 'scented bidis and non-smoking products like hookah, tobacco paste, scented chewable tobacco and zarda', it says, is noteworthy.

Usually a SWOT (strength, weakness, opportunities and threats) analysis is carried out by individual companies or industry associations for different sectors. In case of the tobacco industry, the government carries out the analysis using taxpayers' money. To top it all, one such analysis done by the CTRI on Indian tobacco categorizes the anti-tobacco drive as a 'major threat' to the industry. 'Pressure from the anti-tobacco lobby and stringent regulations being enforced by governments in different countries, including India, are posing a major threat to tobacco production. Campaigns

> Usually a SWOT analysis is carried out by individual companies or industry associations for different sectors. In case of the tobacco industry, the government carries out the analysis using taxpayers' money.

by environmentalists on denundation of forests regarding use of firewood for tobacco curing due to shortage of coal is a concern', the study noted. The CTRI has also identified another threat: 'Large scale smuggling of cigarettes into the country is a major problem faced by the Indian cigarette industry'.[11] It leaves one wondering why the taxpayer's money is being used to enhance the profitability of an industry that is engaged in manufacturing products hazardous to the very health of the taxpayers.

The policy support for the tobacco industry flows from several other wings of the government. Take, for instance, the recommendations made by an expert group of the Planning Commission on agriculture marketing and external trade in 2007.[12] The group recommended a series of sops to boost tobacco exports: enhancing the entitlement under the Duty Entitlement Pass Book (DEPB) scheme on export of tobacco to 12 per cent from 2 per cent; compensating for all taxes paid – indirect or otherwise – at the state or the central level on inputs along the full value chain (farm to export) to make 'exports truly competitive' in relation to other exporting countries; extending the benefit of the drawback on furnace oil consumed by tobacco exporters; giving concessions on service tax; giving exemption from paying service tax on the services rendered abroad; giving exemption from service tax in India; liberal credits for exports, assisting in the development of infrastructure and encouraging R&D activities.

In addition, the government think tank wanted the government to sponsor trips of tobacco trade delegations to major importing countries at regular intervals and publicize Indian tobacco and tobacco products through international tobacco exhibitions and advertisements in international tobacco trade magazines. Subscription to trade-related databases of the US-based Tobacco

Manufacturing Association was also recommended to help the Indian tobacco industry access international tobacco data.

The state's role in nurturing the tobacco industry is all encompassing. It begins with the registration of growers for seedlings and continues in every aspect of the industry – curing, processing, grading, registration of exporters, packers, auctioneers and dealers. The government runs an elaborate system of auction platforms to procure tobacco leaves for private manufacturers. It conducts research on improving crop yields, managing pests, reducing pesticide residues and developing new varieties. It helps the industry in testing, developing new packaging technologies and even conducts market research, and then rewards the best performers. Imagine all this is being done using the taxpayers' money so that private cigarette, bidi, hookah paste and companies manufacturing cut tobacco can sell 'better' products and earn profits. In effect, the Indian taxpayer is funding the growth of an industry which threatens the very health of the taxpayers. India is the only country in the world to have such an elaborate state-funded machinery to promote tobacco.

Stymieing Tobacco Control

Tobacco control activities have been confined to the Ministry of Health and Family Welfare for a long time. The only piece of health legislation available to it was the Cigarettes Act of 1975. The 1980s saw the beginning of anti-tobacco action at the global level with better quantification of the health risks associated with tobacco. The WHO, in its annual resolutions of 1986 and 1990, urged member-states to 'discourage the use of tobacco and impose progressive restrictions on tobacco products' as well as 'take concerted action to eventually eliminate all direct

The government helps the tobacco industry in testing, developing new packaging technologies and even conducts market research, and then rewards the best performers.

and indirect advertising, promotion and sponsorship activities concerning tobacco'. In May 1990, the government banned tobacco-related advertisements on official radio and television channels and also extended statutory health warnings to chewable tobacco. State governments were advised 'to discourage the sale of tobacco products around educational institutions'.

In 1991, the WHO and the health ministry held a series of consultations on the subject 'Tobacco or Health', which made a set of recommendations despite the strong denials by the tobacco lobby about any link between tobacco and human health. The most significant recommendation from this meeting was a proposal to the central government to enact a comprehensive law covering labelling, sale, promotion and consumption of all tobacco products. It also suggested setting up a committee to go into the economics of tobacco, given oft-repeated assertions that its contribution to the national economy was immense. Recognizing tobacco as a 'major health hazard', the conference concluded that 'an integrated educational, legislative and agro-economic strategy with an operational framework and political, administrative, financial and research support, is needed to protect our people from the tobacco menace and move in the direction of a tobacco-free society'. It appeared like an ambitious goal but it did set the agenda for a strong anti-tobacco regime in India for the next two decades.

The first critical step came in September 1993 when the Union Cabinet agreed in principle to enact a comprehensive tobacco law covering all products including cigarettes. It took a full decade to translate this cabinet decision into action. The Cigarettes and Other Tobacco Products (Prohibition of Advertisement and Regulation of Trade and Commerce, Production, Supply and Distribution) Act 2003 was approved by the Parliament and received presidential approval in May 2003.

The period from 1993 to 2003 witnessed the formation of a series of committees and parliamentary panels. Several hearings were also held. But at every stage, the tobacco lobby within and outside the government tried to dilute the recommendations and provisions of the proposed law. The labour ministry raised the issue of the likely impact of the law on the livelihood of people engaged in bidi making. In the expert committee on the economics of tobacco use, the industry used its political clout within the government to increase industry representation by having it reconstituted. Similarly, the proposal to ban the sale of tobacco products within 500 yards of educational institutions was diluted and the distance was reduced to 100 yards. The most significant concession that the tobacco industry succeeded in extracting was keeping the 'point of sale' (PoS) advertising out of the purview of the ban on direct and indirect advertisements of tobacco products.

Despite such efforts by pro-tobacco lobbies, the 2003 Act has turned out to be one of the toughest anti-tobacco laws in the world. It provides for banning all forms of advertising for all tobacco products, banning of sponsorship of events by tobacco companies, prohibition of smoking in public places, restriction of the sale of tobacco products near educational institutions and, above all, makes pictorial health warnings mandatory on all tobacco products. It also makes the indication of tar and nicotine content of tobacco products on packages along with maximum permissible limits mandatory.

Undoubtedly, it is a tough law on paper, but its implementation was again stymied by the clever tactics adopted by the industry and hurdles created within the government.

Surprisingly, the total advertising expenditure of the tobacco industry went up after the ban on advertising was imposed. In the first year after the ban, the ad spend on cigarettes went up to Rs 350 crore from Rs 300 crore in the previous year.[13] The

> The period from 1993 to 2003 witnessed the formation of a series of committees and parliamentary panels. But at every stage, the tobacco lobby within and outside the government tried to dilute the recommendations and provisions of the proposed law.

reason for this increase is the new expenditure on PoS advertising. Manufacturers of chewable tobacco products too increased their budget. The regulations relating to the size and content of PoS advertising are openly flouted. In order to circumvent the ban on advertising, tobacco companies resort to advertising non-tobacco products having the same brand name as tobacco products, also known as surrogate advertising, in all media. All gutka brands are conveniently adopting the surrogate route for advertising by using pan masalas bearing the same brand name. Pan masala, though considered a health hazard, was left out of the ban as it is a non-tobacco product. Though advertising bidis is banned, a prominent bidi brand, 502 Pataka, is being promoted through packaged tea sold under the same brand name. Cigarette companies are also resorting to 'brand stretching and diversification' as exemplified by the Wills Lifestyle Stores opened by ITC, the largest cigarette maker in the country.

The case of pictorial warnings is the most intriguing. The 2003 Act provides for printing of pictorial health warnings on packs of all tobacco products. The objective was to deglamourize smoking and consumption of other tobacco products by printing images of cancers of the lung and mouth. Such warnings are mainly directed at young people as well as those who are not literate – mostly people who use tobacco without being aware of its adverse health impacts.

The first set of rules notified in July 2006 prescribed the printing of 'skull and bone' signs on tobacco packets, with the stipulation that the warning covered 50 per cent of the 'principle display area'. Companies were given a deadline of seven months to implement the warning. In January 2007, the industry sought more time and the deadline was extended to June 2007. In the meantime, around seventy cases were filed by the industry in various courts to keep the new rules sub judice for as long as possible. One of the pleas was that the 'skull and bone' sign they had decided to print conveyed that smoking can kill. In another writ, it was contended that the sign could hurt the feelings of a religious minority.

Several representations were made to the government against the pictorial warnings. Willing lawmakers pleaded for a change in the warnings on the ground that they threatened the bidi industry that supports millions of livelihoods in the country. Prime Minister Manmohan Singh finally yielded and set up a group of ministers (GoM) to arrive at a final decision on the issue. The result was an amendment to the 2003 Act passed by the Parliament in August 2007, making use of the 'skull and bone' sign optional and not mandatory as provided for in the original law. 'Cultural and religious' reasons were cited for doing so. Meanwhile, the industry got a further reprieve from the courts to implement the warnings.

In February 2008, the GoM proposed that cigarette and bidi packs should carry an image of a chest X-ray of a man with cancer. The ministers ignored the fact that only a trained radiologist could understand the significance of such a picture. An image of a scorpion, depicting cancer was suggested to be added on packets of chewable and smokeless tobacco products. The size of the warning was also reduced from 50 per cent to 40 per cent. A new deadline of June 2008 was set for the implementation. It was later extended to 30 November 2008, but in the last week of November the health ministry once again extended it to 31 May 2009. Thus it was postponed for the seventh time. The warnings – mild in content and smaller in size – finally came into force on 1 June 2009. The tobacco industry had won a war by limiting the effectiveness of the pictorial warnings and delaying the law's implementation by several years.

The way politicians colluded with the industry to dilute the warnings is intriguing. The GoM included ministers who had an interest in tobacco and its products. It was a broad representation of the political economy behind tobacco in India. The panel was chaired by the Minister of External Affairs Pranab Mukherjee and included as members Minister of Information and Broadcasting Priya Ranjan Dasmunshi, Minister of State for Labour and Employment Oscar Fernandes, Minister of Commerce and Industry Kamal Nath, Minister of Urban Development S. Jaipal Reddy and Minister of

Health and Family Welfare Ambumani Ramadoss. Both Mukherjee and Dasmunshi were elected from constituencies in West Bengal where bidi making is a major vocation. Other members – Fernandes and Reddy – represented two of the largest tobacco-producing states – Karnataka and Andhra Pradesh. Fernandes was elected from Udupi in Mangalore, which is a major bidi-producing centre in south India. As commerce minister, Kamal Nath had openly advocated the welfare of the tobacco industry, putting it at par with other commercial crops such as tea and coconut.[14]

The most vocal opposition to the strong pictorial warnings came from Mukherjee who represented the Jangipur constituency in the Lok Sabha. In one of the meetings, he articulated the industry demands this way: 'A number of representations have been received from the bidi industry that employs a large number of workers from the weaker sections of society. The basic issues raised by the bidi industry relate to the size, colour and obnoxious nature of the pictorial warnings.' The pictorial warnings, in his view, could not be 'totally repulsive'. He also noted that the skull and bone picture was 'objectionable to a minority community'. Regarding the size of the warning, he argued, it would 'cover the entire bidi pack, leaving no space for printing the manufacturer's name.'[15]

Pressure to tone down the pictorial warnings came from several other quarters within the government including Civil Aviation Minister Praful Patel, who is known as the bidi king of Vidarbha. He owns one of Maharashtra's biggest bidi and tobacco-derivatives businesses, according to details of his assets filed with the Election Commission of India. Several cabinet ministers, state chief ministers and members of Parliament took up the cause of the tobacco industry.

Health minister A. Ramadoss was flooded with letters from cabinet colleagues and politicians – all pleading on behalf of the tobacco industry.[16] They wanted a postponement of the health warnings. Agriculture minister Sharad Pawar feared that the new warnings would 'throw a large number of female (bidi) workers out of jobs'. Commerce and industry minister Kamal Nath too wanted a postponement. Pranab Mukherjee asked Ramadoss to 'review the decision in view of the memorandum submitted by the Bidi Industry Federation'. Congress leader Salman Khursheed, writing on behalf of the Tobacco Manufacturers Association, wanted the health ministry to drop the 'extreme skull-bones icon'. Janardhan Poojary, a member of the Upper House, even went to the extent of saying 'bidi is relatively safer than cigarette and liquor'.

Tamil Nadu Chief Minister M. Karunanidhi wanted the health ministry to defer the implementation of the new rules, saying that 'the move threatened the livelihood of 1.5 million bidi workers in the state'. His West Bengal counterpart Buddhadeb Bhattacharjee noted that the bidi industry provided employment to 10 lakh people in Bengal and wanted the decision 'reviewed so that lakhs of people engaged in the bidi industry do not lose their livelihood'. Andhra Pradesh Chief Minister Y.S. Rajasekhar Reddy led an all-party delegation to meet the prime minister seeking withdrawal of the health warnings. The AP state assembly even passed a resolution seeking exemption from printing the warnings on the bidi packets. It was pointed out that the bidi workers would lose their jobs if manufacturers started printing harsher warnings on the packs.

In all, Ramadoss received about 100 letters from the who's who of Indian politics lobbying for the tobacco industry. Just two members of Parliament – Rajeev Chandrasekhar and N.K. Somani – spoke in favour of the new warnings. Given this kind of political pressure and feeling isolated, Ramadoss went public in November 2007, saying that five chief ministers and 150 members of Parliament had written to him to dilute the pictorial warnings. After several rounds of deliberations in the GoM headed by the pro-tobacco

The AP state assembly even passed a resolution seeking an exemption from printing the warnings on the bidi packets. It was pointed out that bidi workers would lose their jobs if manufacturers started printing harsher warnings on these packs.

Mukherjee, it was decided that a milder set of warnings would be notified in March 2008. But this finally came into effect in June 2009.

This was not the end of the story. The anti-tobacco law requires the warnings to be changed every year from a set of graphics. So the health ministry again proposed a set of harsher warnings in March 2010 so that they could come into effect from June 2010. The ministry felt that 'the existing warnings do not convey the anti-tobacco message in an effective manner and are, rather, hardly understood by the community at large.' But once again, the tobacco lobbies within and outside the government became active. Law minister Veerappa Moily wrote to the health minister on behalf of an entity called the Pan Shop Owners Association of India, which argued that new health warnings on tobacco products would spell 'poverty, starvation and death' for small retailers. This time, however, the tobacco lobby received a patient hearing in the health ministry. The tide had turned in favour of the tobacco industry after the 2009 general elections, which saw a new health minister at the helm. Ramadoss was replaced by Congress veteran Ghulam Nabi Azad.

Azad promptly intervened and directed that the March 2010 notification for harsher warnings be kept in abeyance. However, the tobacco control wing in the ministry said there would be a backlash, pointing out that the move was 'certain to attract major criticism not only from anti-tobacco activists and media but possibly also in courts and the Parliament… We should be very careful about withdrawing the newer and harsher pictorial drawings. Our task in the Ministry of Health is to actively discourage smokers and horrible pictures of mouths and lungs with cancerous growths are an effective deterrent. We need not plead the case of the Ministry of Commerce or the Ministry of Labour.'[17] The then health secretary Sujatha Rao conveyed to Azad that 'in view of the direct adverse impact of tobacco products on cancer and cardiovascular diseases and the extremely pro-active stand taken by the former minister (A. Ramadoss) on this issue, it would be advisable not to give the impression that the

Azad rattled off the same arguments that the tobacco lobby had been advancing for years – when rape, murder and other ills can be shown in movies, why ban scenes that show people smoking?

ministry is backtracking.' A compromise was then arrived at. It was decided not to set aside the notification, as directed by Azad, yet harsher pictorial warnings were not implemented from 1 June 2010 as per the notification. Instead, another order was issued to permit tobacco product manufacturers to continue with the existing milder warnings till 1 December 2010. As a result, the tobacco industry got yet another reprieve.

A ban on on-screen smoking was another anti-tobacco measure that was strongly opposed within the government. The opposition came during the tenure of two successive I&B ministers – Dasmunshi and Jaipal Reddy – both known for their lenient views towards the tobacco industry and both ex-members of the crucial GoM on pictorial warnings. The film fraternity too – led by film-maker Mahesh Bhatt – opposed the move. Kannada film actor and Minister of State for Information and Broadcasting Ambareesh too, protested, saying the ban would interfere with the 'creative freedom' of film-makers.

Yet again, Azad saw no rationale behind the ban on smoking scenes on the silver screen, ignoring research findings that it was capable of influencing young minds to smoke. For tobacco companies, this kind of promotion was a godsend since all other forms of tobacco advertising had been banned. Azad rattled off the same arguments that the tobacco lobby had been advancing for years – when rape, murder and other ills can be shown in movies, why ban scenes that show people smoking? Finally, in August 2012, it was decided to let films show such scenes but with health warnings running on a scroll. Ironically, the health ministry agreed to pay for the production cost of showing these scrolls and health messages. Its earlier decision that all films with smoking scenes be given the U/A certificate by the Censor Board was also reversed.

Smokeless Tobacco Flourishes

While smoking came under the health scanner in India with the statutory health warnings in 1975, smokeless tobacco continued to have no checks till the mid-1990s. The government made no effort to either curtail production of pan masala and gutka or push printing of health warnings on packs, despite the phenomenal growth of the industry in the 1980s. The first move to bring chewable tobacco products under the purview of a law was spurred by a judgment of the Rajasthan High Court in April 1994. The case related to another tobacco product – a tobacco toothpaste manufactured by a company based in Bundi in Rajasthan. The company had challenged the ban on manufacturing imposed by the state government. The court upheld the ban, and, in the judgment, also directed the central government 'to appoint a committee of experts regarding the use of tobacco in pan masala, gutka etc., and its effect on public health.' The government, the court said, should take steps to prohibit the manufacture of these items if the committee recommended that these products are injurious to public health. It also directed that such a decision be taken within six months.

The Central Committee for Food Standards (CCFS) – a technical panel working under the Ministry of Health – in its meeting held on 26 and 27 November 1997, passed a resolution recommending a nationwide ban on pan masala, gutka and other chewing tobacco products. The resolution said, 'On the basis of literatures/studies available so far on the adverse effects of consumption of pan masala containing tobacco, gutka, chewing tobacco, the experts strongly recommend that use of chewing tobacco in pan masala, gutka or as an ingredient in any food item or as such, should be prohibited as consumption of these articles is definitely injurious to public health.'

When the panel examined the scientific evidence, it came across a study from Ahmedabad that showed that smokers suffer from cancer after exposure over a period of fifteen to sixty-eight years, while gutka chewers were diagnosed within about ten years of exposure. Among patients who died, the average age of patients who smoked was fifty-four years, but for gutka chewers it was forty-one years.[18] Members of CCFS also wanted other non-smoking products to be banned because women often used them, while they avoided smoking due to social disapproval.

The CCFS's decision sent the chewable tobacco industry into a tizzy. B.K. Das, president of Bharatiya Supari Zarda Trade Association, went to the press saying the government would lose revenues of over Rs 700 crore if the ban came into effect. Chewable tobacco products, in his view, had been singled out on 'baseless grounds' while cigarettes attracted no such action.[19] Concerns were also raised about the potential loss of employment for the people employed in the industry.

The health ministry circulated the CCFS recommendation to all ministries concerned with the tobacco industry. As expected, some of them expressed reservations on an immediate ban 'because of the large implications for tobacco growers and those involved in the manufacture, production and sale of tobacco, tobacco products and other ensuing consequences.' Instead of a ban on manufacture and sale, the health ministry felt that steps like statutory warnings on pan masala and gutka packs and restrictions on advertising were better options.

The government's view was amplified in an affidavit filed in the Mumbai High Court by J.S. Chaudhary, the then deputy secretary in the Ministry of Health. The government, it said, was 'aware of the ill effects of pan masala containing tobacco, gutka, chewable tobacco, as well as other tobacco products' and was following a policy 'to discourage their consumption and restrict their sale.' The

Instead of a ban on manufacture and sale, the health ministry felt that steps like statutory warnings on pan masala and gutka packs and restrictions on advertising were better options.

strategy was to first 'moderate and discourage the consumption of different kinds of tobacco products' and to tackle the issue in a phased manner, 'taking into consideration various related factors'. Clearly, many within the government were not in favour of imposing a ban on pan masala and gutka. Not only this, the statutory warning proposed by CCFS – 'Pan masala is harmful if taken regularly' – was diluted to 'Pan masala may be harmful' by the Committee of Secretaries.[20]

In July 2002, Maharashtra banned the sale of pan masala and gutka in the state and the ban was challenged by the industry in the Mumbai High Court. The Food and Drug Administration revealed that it had seized some samples that contained 2 to 5 per cent of magnesium carbonate. If someone consumed five sachets of two grams each, they could be consuming 200 mg to 500 mg of magnesium carbonate per day. Over a period of time, this could lead to acute hypermagnesaemia, which could cause hypotension due to peripheral vasodilation, neuromuscular blockade, muscle weakness, respiratory depression, cardiac arrhythmia and even cardiac arrest. In addition, Indian studies cited by the FDA to justify the ban showed adverse impacts including cancer and heart disease.

A study conducted by the Indian Council of Medical Research on five popular brands of gutka revealed the presence of polyaromatic hydrocarbons, nitrosamines and toxic metals like lead, cadmium and nickel.[21] It pointed out that frequent intake of pan masala every day can initially lead to a rise in blood pressure for some days and ultimately cause hypertension. The finding was that pan masala consumption poses significant long-term cardiovascular risk.

Within a month of the Maharashtra ban, an interesting development took place in Uttar Pradesh. The Allahabad High Court imposed a ban on the manufacture and sale of pan masala and gutka in the state during the hearing of a case related to spurious pan masala. It was a big blow to the industry as all major manufacturers were based in Kanpur and Noida and it was challenged in the Supreme Court, which promptly granted a stay on the High Court order.

A curious side of the legal battle of the chewable tobacco industry was that it carefully chose top lawyers from different political parties to defend its case. In the Mumbai High Court, pan masala and gutka manufacturers were defended by Congress party politician Kapil Sibal, who was then a member of the Upper House of Parliament. The special leave petition filed by the industry in the Supreme Court was argued against by Arun Jaitley, who was chief spokesperson and general secretary of the BJP which was in power at the Centre. Sibal's defence against the ban on manufacture and sale of pan masala and gutka in Maharashtra was that one cannot just prohibit such products on the basis of 'long years of consumption, the frequency of consumption and the tendency of being addicted. There is hardly any manufactured food for human consumption which does not have any deleterious long-term effect on human health based on the pattern of consumption.'[22]

Gutka makers challenged the ban on manufacturing in the Supreme Court, which, in August 2004, set aside the ban on technical grounds of the State not having the powers to prohibit manufacturing of pan masala and gutka under the Prevention of Food Adulteration Act of 1954. Such powers, the court said, were vested only in the central government. This judgment, however, was not an endorsement of the safety of chewable tobacco products.

In 2006, the health ministry decided to prohibit the manufacturing of gutka and pan masala. It notified the Prevention of Food Adulteration (Amendment) Rules, 2006, prohibiting the use of tobacco and nicotine as ingredients in any food product. Ramadoss wanted to use this provision to ban the manufacturing of chewable tobacco products as they were

> A curious side of the legal battle of the chewable tobacco industry was that it carefully chose top lawyers from different political parties to defend its case.

classified as 'food products' under the law. As predicted, manufacturers challenged the amendment in various high courts. After a few hearings, all these petitions were transferred to the Supreme Court in 2009. The court asked the government to file a detailed report on the adverse health effects of chewable products. A report submitted by the Ministry of Health and the National Institute of Health and Family Welfare revealed the presence of over 3095 chemical components in chewable tobacco products including twenty-eight proven carcinogens. The most abundant group of carcinogens is the tobacco-specific N-nitrosamines (TSNA). The report attributed 90 per cent of oral cancer cases in the country to tobacco.

In August 2011, the Food Safety & Standards Authority of India (FSSAI) issued a notification stating that no food article shall contain tobacco or nicotine in the products. The Regulation says 'product not to contain any substance which may be injurious to health. Tobacco and nicotine shall not be used as ingredients in any food products'. Once again, the onus of pushing the ban on gutka shifted to the central government. The final directive came from the Supreme Court that gutka was a food item and as per the food law no food product could contain tobacco. Based on this ruling, twenty-six states banned the manufacture and sale of gutka at the end of 2013.

Tobacco is being consumed in different forms – mainly hookah or shisha –in urban India. In the rural areas of north India, hookah has been prevalent for a long time but its use was traditionally restricted to certain communities. It has emerged as a new form of tobacco consumption in urban areas too as restrictions on tobacco products were imposed in 2000. Urban youth were led to believe that hookah was safe because all the toxic elements get filleted when the smoke passes through water.

Hookah became hip. It moved from the village chaupal to five-star hotels and standalone tobacco consumption parlours known as 'hookah bars'. The youth, including a large number of women, who would otherwise shun smoking, flock hookah bars. They

> The youth, including a large number of women, who would otherwise shun smoking, flock hookah bars. They seem to be convinced about what the tobacco industry says: hookahs are tobacco-free.

seem to be convinced about the tobacco industry's statement that hookahs are tobacco-free. Hookah tobacco paste is often mixed with sweetening agents like molasses, honey, dried fruits and flavouring essences. Those who smoke hookah insist that it is 'not as injurious to health as cigarettes, chewable tobacco, chocolates, and even tea and coffee.'[23] Public health experts, on the other hand, said, 'hookah smoking could also become a gateway to cigarette smoking' and it may 'lead to cigarette smoking and a lifelong addiction to smoking tobacco.'[24]

Like other tobacco products, hookah also has benign state support. As already discussed, Indian government agencies promote growth and export of tobacco including hookah tobacco. So this tobacco also enjoys all the subsidies and incentives like the other forms of tobacco. Hookah tobacco is an important product for export from India. Around 10,656 tonnes of hookah paste was exported in 2007–08, representing 34.7 per cent of the quantity of tobacco exported.[25] Some of it may be now flowing into the domestic market, given the rising number of hookah bars in the country. The 2003 tobacco control law bans smoking in public places, and restricts smoking to a separate room in restaurants. Hookah bars are exploiting this as a loophole because they advertise themselves as hookah parlours and not as a restaurant. This circumvents the need for a separate smoking room as required under the law. Hookahs are sold without any health warnings because the windpipe contraption (hardware) is tobacco free. It is the tobacco paste that makes hookah a tobacco 'product' and users almost invariably do not see the packaging of the paste which may contain the mandatory health warning.

Conclusions

It is clear that the tobacco industry in India comprising products like cigarette, bidi and gutka has not only received official patronage from government agencies dedicated to the development of the tobacco industry but it also enjoys widespread support in other sections of the government as well as from people of influence across the political spectrum. Political support towards tobacco is often justified in the name of 'livelihood' of the people engaged in bidi and retail trade. But such a justification ignores thousands who die of tobacco-related deaths every year. The Parliament and state assemblies have members lobbying for the tobacco industry. Such lobbies, however, don't exist for commodities that promote health products, like fresh fruits or healthy foods. The central government has a Tobacco Board but no Health Promotion Board. The government does not give subsidies nor does it hand out awards to the best-performing cultivators of fruits or healthy foods, but it awards tobacco farmers and cigarette companies.

The efforts of the health ministry to curb tobacco consumption and restrict the industry's growth with the help of advertising bans and health warnings have been half-hearted and often sabotaged by influential ministers in the government and, at times, even by health ministers. The tobacco industry is seen as a major revenue earner and employment generator. Policymakers and politicians have ignored the economic fallout of the adverse health impacts of tobacco on the exchequer and the loss of many productive lives on the nation's economy. A tough anti-tobacco law exists on paper, but what is lacking is the necessary mechanism and political will required to enforce it.

The efforts of the health ministry to curb tobacco consumption and restrict the industry's growth with the help of advertising bans and health warnings have been half-hearted.

Call to Action

> 'Many people believe that if individuals develop chronic disease as a result of unhealthy "lifestyles", they have no one to blame but themselves. The truth is that individual responsibility can have its full effect only where individuals have equitable access to a healthy life, and are supported to make healthy choices. Governments have a crucial role to play in improving the health and well-being of populations.'
>
> – WHO

Just as proper hygiene, good sanitation and powerful drugs helped us overcome the challenges posed by communicable diseases, nipping the risk factors in the bud can help us tackle lifestyle diseases. To prevent malaria from spreading and also in order to eradicate it, we need to stop the breeding of mosquitoes. We know the bug that causes tuberculosis and how it is transmitted. But in the case of heart disease, there is no bug or vector that requires eradication. It is a host of risk factors, which to most people are like an amorphous entity. Factors like 'healthy food' and 'physical activity' are open to different interpretations by different people and in different cultural contexts.

It is a complex web of environmental, behavioural and societal factors that influences to a great extent the prevalence of the determinants leading to heart disease in any country. Yes, it is possible for us to control some of these since it is in our own hands to decide what we should or shouldn't eat or whether we should exercise. At the same time, it is true that an individual can't take such decisions and act in an environment that is not stimulating or does not offer healthy choices. Changing human behaviour is a complex issue. That's why mere education and awareness campaigns don't yield the desired results. Experts have pointed out that a major part of human behaviour is automatic, cued by environmental stimuli and results in actions that are largely not based on conscious reflection.[1]

We opt for healthy choices only after some ailment has come knocking on our doors. But when the scale of the problem reaches epic proportions, efforts at an individual level may not be able to make a dent in the society's overall disease burden. That's the reason why India needs change on a larger scale along with individual prevention and efforts in clinical settings to control and prevent the tide of heart disease. Instead of solely depending on the individual to take action, we can provide positive stimuli by tweaking food and built environments so that it becomes easy for us to make healthy choices.

We have seen how India's food and physical environments are changing and how state policies are making them unfriendly for the heart. How these environments are shaped depends largely on policies the government adopts. The WHO has aptly summarized the situation: 'Many people believe that if individuals develop chronic disease as a result of unhealthy "lifestyles", they have no one to blame but themselves. The truth is that individual responsibility can work effectively only where individuals have equitable access to a healthy life, and are supported to make healthy choices. Governments have a crucial role to play in improving the health and well-being of populations.'[2]

India needs change on a larger scale along with individual prevention and efforts in clinical settings to control and prevent the tide of heart disease.

Undoubtedly, it is for an individual to decide whether to consume a particular food item or a beverage, or whether to walk and use public transport or drive to work. This decision-making process, however, is not always rational. Given the complexity of the environment and the choices it poses, 'many of these decisions are automatic and subconscious.' For instance, experts have argued, excessive food consumption occurs in ways that defy personal insight or are below individual awareness.[3] While there can be interventions such as health promotion, awareness and education aimed at motivating individual behavioural changes, it is policy interventions (such as increasing the costs of unhealthy food, expanding public transport facilities, enforcing healthy land-use policies) that can influence environmental drivers and result in population-wide changes. In the case of obesity, for example, almost all interventions needed to reverse the obesity-causing environment will have to be policy led. Compared to health education and awareness, policy-led solutions that apply to the whole environment tend to be sustainable and systemic. Such solutions, however, are generally difficult to implement because of strong political and business interests.

In the Indian scenario, changes in public policy are a prerequisite for a healthy nation, because it is the state policies that influence the behaviour of people in relation to three major risk factors of heart disease: unhealthy diet, tobacco consumption and physical inactivity. It would be absurd if we expect individuals to change their behaviour for the better while all the state does is promote and subsidize unhealthy food and tobacco through public policies that help create environments that make it difficult for people to eat healthy or undertake physical activity. Isn't it the responsibility of the state to help its citizens make healthy choices? Why should the state make the

It would be absurd if we expect individuals to change their behaviour for the better while all the state does is promote and subsidize unhealthy food and tobacco through public policies.

process of opting for healthy choices so difficult for its citizens? A responsible government should help people make a smooth transition towards a healthy lifestyle.

Public policies in India in several sectors are directly and indirectly contributing to situations where the risk of heart disease is enhanced. This is despite the increasing scientific evidence about how public policy can change behaviour, reduce the risk of heart disease and ultimately the disease burden and mortality rates. The experience of some advanced Western countries is testimony to this.

In several countries, the application of available scientific knowledge and evidence has led to a sharp decline in the heart disease rate and deaths occurring due to it. For example, heart disease death rates have fallen by up to 70 per cent in the last three decades in Australia, Canada, the United Kingdom and the United States.[4] Middle-income countries, such as Poland, have also reported large gains in recent years. Such improvements, according to an analysis by the WHO, were realized largely as a result of the implementation of strategies that combine both the population in its entirety and individuals, and by focusing on a reduction or modification of the underlying risk factors. From 1970 to 2000, the WHO estimated that 14 million cardiovascular disease deaths were averted in the US, while three million lives were saved in the UK during the same period.

The evidence from Finland is more striking. Both heart disease and stroke mortality have declined by 75 to 80 per cent since the 1970s. This has been attributed to the sustained efforts to support a more healthy diet (a reduction in saturated fat and sodium consumption; an increase in fruit and vegetable consumption), discouraging tobacco consumption and promoting the use of medicines that reduce the risk of heart disease. Less than 25 per cent of the drop was on account of treatment. The change was a result of joint action by the government, health professionals, farmers, food companies and local voluntary bodies. Between 1972 and 2007, blood cholesterol declined by 21 per cent among men and by 23 per cent among women; systolic blood pressure declined by 10.1 mmHg in men and by 18.6 mmHg in women; and smoking among men declined from 52 to 31 per cent in the North Karelia Province.[5]

In the US, nearly half the reduction can be attributed to population-level changes in the risk factors such as tobacco use, diet and physical activity, while the rest can be attributed to improvements in treatment and healthcare facilities.[6] Over the past half century, health benefits like a 50 per cent reduction in smoking and a 30-point decrease in cholesterol levels could be seen after two major risk factors were tackled. It is no more fashionable to smoke in a major part of the Western world.[7] Along with a reduction in the predisposing factor, advances made in bypass surgery and new medications have helped save many lives. Health promotion among individuals during routine clinical check-ups and through sustained mass health-awareness campaigns are helpful too.

The current approach to tackle the heart disease problem in India is flawed. It only focuses on the treatments in tertiary-care hospitals. Little attention is paid to prevention at any level. Even if the government understands and appreciates the need for prevention, the task is left to the health ministry. The realization that this cannot be achieved only by the health sector or the health ministry is yet to dawn upon policymakers. This exercise should involve several ministries in the government since most of the risk factors cut across multiple sectors. The health sector too needs to initiate specific measures since it is not fully geared to handle lifestyle diseases.

Policy Changes in Non-health Sectors

India needs carefully designed policies and health interventions that will cut across sectors. A consultation organized by the Ministry of Health in 2006 noted that 'appropriate and well-designed policies can have powerful, far-reaching and long-term effects at the population level.' It was pointed out that essential prerequisites for a prevention strategy would be cooperation and partnership among sixteen ministries of the Government of India – health and family welfare, human resources development, industry and commerce, finance, urban development, rural development, women and child welfare, food and agriculture, food processing, environment and forests, roads and transport, labour, social welfare, home affairs, information technology and science and technology – besides national and state commissions for women as well as child development. This only points towards the magnitude of the task at hand and to the fact that though heart disease is a health problem, the Ministry of Health is just a cog in the wheel of the solution.

> The current approach to tackle the heart disease problem in India is flawed. Little attention is paid to prevention at any level. Even if the government understands and appreciates the need for prevention, the task is left to the health ministry.

Let's start with the food environment because important interventions are needed in this sector. Providing healthier food choices to people and preventing unhealthy changes in dietary patterns require strong policy interventions, and the rationale for doing so exists in the form of a large body of evidence. Put simply, we need policies that will encourage consumption of fresh fruits and vegetables, whole grains, whole pulses, nuts as well as fish. Regulatory interventions are needed to moderate consumption of saturated fats, salt and refined carbohydrates, while the use of artificial trans-fats should be completely stopped.

Food consumption patterns – the type, quality and quantity of food – are determined by relative food pricing in markets. 'Systematically altering relative prices of different food items will favourably affect food consumption, which will bring down obesity, blood pressure, serum cholesterol and blood glucose at the population level, and thereby save millions of people from chronic diseases.' This was a conclusion of a scientific review published in the journal *Current Science* in 2009.[8] Food prices, along with the shopping environment, significantly contribute towards people's weight problems and obesity, experts argued. Translating this into action will require active cooperation and policy changes brought into effect by the ministries of health, food, agriculture, food processing, roads and transport, finance and several other wings of the government such as agriculture prices commission, food safety authority and the planning commission. Above all, it will require necessary political will since pricing of commodities is always a political decision in India.

Edible oil production and pricing is a key area where policy action can influence consumption patterns. Scientific studies have shown that blood cholesterol levels are largely determined by the proportion of dietary energy derived from trans-fats, saturated fats and polyunsaturated fats and have to be controlled in order to reduce the refined carbohydrates. So, in effect, diet dictates cholesterol levels, which increases the risk of heart disease. A meta-analysis of several international studies showed that 80 per cent of variation in heart disease is due to changes in blood cholesterol levels. Average blood cholesterol concentration can accurately predict the occurrence of heart disease in a population. A rise of 23.4 mg/dl was found to be associated with a 38 per cent increase in ischaemic heart disease deaths, while an equivalent fall resulted in a 25 to 30 per cent fall in the incidence of the disease within five years.[9] Conversely, the occurrence of the disease has fallen by the predicted level in countries where average cholesterol concentrations have come down. And this dip benefits the entire population. In addition, according to cardiologists, diet determines how much antioxidants and other nutrients our body receives through fresh fruits and vegetables.

Scientific studies have shown that blood cholesterol levels are largely determined by the proportion of dietary energy derived from trans-fats, saturated fats and refined carbohydrates.

Tropical oils have worried many public health researchers because they increase the risk of cardiovascular disease. Healthy oils can be defined as those that have zero commercially introduced trans-fatty acids and which are low in saturated fatty acids and are high in mono- and polyunsaturated fatty acids. Nutritionally, oleic acid and linoleic acid are considered the most useful mono and polyunsaturated fatty acids respectively. 'In order to be truly effective, low and middle-income countries that have high levels of oil consumption will need to develop affordable supplies of healthy oils at prices that are competitive with tropical oils [such as palm oil],' an expert group said.[10]

The government needs to give up policies that encourage import of cheap but unhealthy oils, and devise mechanisms to provide necessary fiscal and non-fiscal incentives to encourage production of healthy oils based on scientific evidence and not on price alone. A long-term plan should be formulated to encourage the production of healthy oilseeds and phasing out of unhealthy oils. Such a shift will also call for serious engagement with the highly competitive edible oil industry.

The example of Mauritius is often cited by health experts to prove the point about how policy measures can result in handsome health dividends. The government in this island nation decided in 1987 – through an act of policy – to change the composition of commonly used cooking oil from mostly palm oil (high in saturated fatty acids) to wholly soybean oil (high in unsaturated fatty acids). Over the years, this change led to a significant reduction in the blood cholesterol levels of its people.

The extent to which the food processing industry, which includes aerated sugary drinks like colas, needs encouragement, tax breaks, subsidies and other state support – has to be carefully reviewed. Why should makers of sugary syrups and sodas be given tax breaks in India when countries in the West are thinking of imposing 'soda taxes'? Should potato chips, which are high in trans-fats, saturated fatty acids and sodium, continue to enjoy low rates of taxation and indirect subsidies provided to the food processing industries? These are some important questions policymakers need to address.

The markets – owing to tax regimes and other factors – are so skewed in favour of ultra processed food items that are rich in sugar, fats and salt that it is cheaper to buy a packet of potato chips or masala snack than bananas or a packet of healthy snack like chana. Should rice mills be given fiscal incentives and subsidies when scientific evidence points to white rice (compared to unpolished or brown rice) contributing to the onset of diabetes, which, we all know, is one of the root causes of heart disease? If the incentives granted to rice mills are withdrawn and brown or unpolished rice is promoted, we would enjoy tremendous health benefits.

Salt intake is yet another area where carefully crafted policy interventions are needed. All traditional Indian diets are rich in salt. In addition to the salt used in daily cooking, Indians also consume papads, pickles, churans, and salty snacks. Table salt, too, has become fashionable after it was aggressively marketed by some food companies. The traditional salt intake is being supplemented by salt in ready-to-eat foods, soups and a host of snacks like potato chips. All anecdotal data leads to the conclusion that the salt intake of Indians is going up. A study conducted in Chennai found the average daily salt intake to be 8.5 grams, which is much higher than the WHO standard of 5 grams. Clearly, policies are needed to reduce or restrict the salt intake, and to encourage the production of low-sodium salt.

Since traditional cooking methods and eating habits cannot be changed through a policy diktat, salt reduction strategies would have to be directed at processed, ready-to-eat and restaurant food. Along with such measures, experts have suggested that documentation of salt intake among populations living in different agro-climatic zones of India is necessary so that region-specific guidelines for salt intake could be developed.[11]

Since food served in restaurants and in street-side stalls is a major source of salt consumption, an example from Singapore is worth examining. Just as studies found a high intake of salt among Chennai residents, the mean salt intake for an average adult Singaporean was found to be 9 grams (which translates into 3525 mg of sodium) each day. When the health authorities found that 90 per cent of Singaporeans exceed the daily recommended level of salt consumption, they decided to take population-wide steps to control the menace.

Singapore's health promotion board launched a programme to promote the availability of healthier choices in hawker centres, food courts, restaurants, workplaces, homes and made healthier packaged products available. More than 5700 stalls at 140 food centres in the city-state display 'Ask For' labels, inviting customers to ask for more vegetables, less fat, oil, sugar and salt in their food or drinks. Restaurants displaying the 'Hearty' logo feature dishes prepared using heart-smart diet guidelines. Under a voluntary scheme called Healthier Hawker Food Programme, hawkers have agreed to partially replace ingredients such as coconut milk with evaporated milk, use fibre-added vermicelli instead of those made with refined flour, and replace high-saturated-fat cooking oil with specially formulated reduced saturated fat oil.

Similarly, under the Healthier Dining Programme, restaurants prepare dishes from existing menus with less oil, salt, sugar and some items with additional fruits and vegetables. To identify the healthier dishes offered by participating outlets, customers have to look out for the 'Healthier Choice' logo. Some even offer 'Healthier Children's Menus'. The 'Healthy Eating Out' guidelines issued by the Board do not hesitate in making bold recommendations such as 'Order juice, low-fat milk or plain water instead of soda drinks'. This way, the state is proactively encouraging healthier food and discouraging junk food as aerated drinks.

The US FDA announced a drastic measure on 1 April 2011: new regulations making mandatory 'calorie labelling on menus and menu boards in chain restaurants, retail food establishments, and vending machines'.[12] These regulations make it compulsory for chain restaurants running more than twenty retail outlets under the same name to disclose calorie and other nutrition information of food items listed on menus. The idea is to provide consumers consistent and easy-to-understand nutrition information when they make their own food choices.

Unlike Singapore or the US, the Indian government's response in this regard has been patchy. In India, there is no voluntary programme or regulatory restriction on the quality of food served in restaurants as well as by roadside hawkers or in food courts. The unorganized food sector – mainly consisting of street vendors – is large and 'forms the mainstay of at least one meal consumed outside home, especially amongst people from the middle and low socio-economic backgrounds in urban areas.'[13] Of late, it has been noticed that the poor are not the only consumers of street food. Middle-class youngsters, professional workers and students too are flocking to roadside eateries for quick bites in cities. The food dished out by street vendors is cheap but unhealthy since it is cooked in oil that is used and reused, making it highly toxic. It also has a liberal helping of salt. That's why it is important to design interventions targeted at this sector.

A project was initiated by the Ministry of Food Processing in 2008 for street vendors and the FSSAI issued guidelines for street food. Focus was on the improvement of the quality of street food in terms of hygiene and not health and nutrition. The FSSAI guidelines make general suggestions for street food vendors such as 'proper quality/branded oils/fats should be used for food preparation, frying etc.,' and 'use packaged oil only'. The use of healthier oils and less salt is not particularly emphasized in the food safety guidelines.

In the context of the overall food environment, street vendors have a key role to play in the food chain in urban areas. They are not only vending cheap food to millions of poor Indians every day, but are also a preferred source of vegetables and fruits for millions of poor as well as the middle class and rich Indians. It is estimated that in several Indian cities, street vendors account for 2 per cent of the population. The total number of street vendors in the country is estimated to be 10 million. In the policy apparatus, street vendors have been recognized as 'a very important segment of the unorganized sector in the country'.[14] Urban vending, according to the National Policy for Urban Street Vendors, is not only a source of employment but also provides affordable services and products to the majority of the urban population. The main reason for patronizing hawkers is that fruits and vegetables sold by them are fresh besides being cheap.

Street food hawkers, therefore, need to be actively engaged from two public health perspectives – modulating the salt and fatty oil intake in food stuff they sell and encouraging the vending of fresh fruits and vegetables. They need to be particularly discouraged from using cooking oils with trans-fats. Yet, there is no official plan related to street vendors. Many city administrations, police, big shop owners and people who travel by road consider them a mere nuisance. The police harass the vendors, while city administrations design policies to discourage them. Centrally funded schemes such as the Jawaharlal Nehru Urban Renewal Mission (JNURM) are directed at converting Indian cities into 'world class cities' and one of the major components is clearing up slum clusters.

The opening up of food retail chains, which stock cold-stored local fruits, vegetables and exotic fruits run by large Indian companies, have emerged as a threat to traditional fruit and vegetable sellers. A survey of street vendors conducted near two new malls in Mumbai revealed a 60 to 80 per cent decline in sales by hawkers and small shops after the malls entered the business. Most of the decline was reported in grocery items, fruits and vegetables.[15] At the same

Street food hawkers, therefore, need to be actively engaged from two public health perspectives – modulating the salt and fatty oil intake in food stuff they sell and encouraging the vending of fresh fruits and vegetables. They need to be particularly discouraged from using cooking oils with trans-fats.

time, giant food companies that market packaged fruit juices see street stalls selling fresh fruit juice as their 'biggest enemy'.[16] It is feared that the entry of multinationals in organized retail could further impact small food vendors who act as the primary link between producers (and suppliers of fruits, vegetables and agricultural commodities) and urban consumers.

Food marketing and labelling play a central role in influencing food choices. Nutritional food labelling was made mandatory by the government in 2008, but there are loopholes. In a country where illiteracy rates are high and health awareness is low even among literates, the nutrition labels printed on food products have far too technical information. A survey carried out by market research firm Nielsen in 2008 showed that only 59 per cent of Indians understand nutritional panels and labels on food packaging.[17]

Most people find it difficult to make sense of technical nutritional information on food labels, even though they may be precise and are based on the norms that are laid down. Instead, simple colour-coded labels on basic nutrients and health implications concerning the food product could be more useful in providing the information. Labels should be made more graphic and comprehensible. Continuous research needs to be done on how these labels are being interpreted by people. The packs are too cluttered with promotional information and nutritional data. Experts have suggested front-of-the pack traffic-light nutrition labelling for food products.

The most serious lacunae in food labelling rules is that the food manufacturers are allowed to make nutritional, health and risk reduction claims based on their ingredients. Big food companies – which follow more stringent rules in international markets – are misleading consumers in India with labels such as 'heart healthy', 'fat free' or

Most people find it difficult to make sense of technical nutritional information on food labels, even though they may be precise and based on the norms that are laid down.

'sugar free'. Experts point out that 'it is a myth that if a label says "cholesterol free", the product will not affect the blood cholesterol levels. Even if a product has zero grams of cholesterol (for example, most products from plants), it can still negatively affect blood cholesterol levels if it contains a high amount of trans- or saturated fats, which can give bad cholesterol a boost.'[18]

While the presence of trans-fats has to be declared on the label, the government has refrained from fixing a limit on its permissible levels. The labelling rules need to be reviewed, made more accessible and tougher. Health and nutrition claims shouldn't be allowed on labels. Advertising of junk foods targeted at children needs to be restricted. Like tobacco advertising, marketing and promotion of unhealthy food in schools, co-promotion and branding with other products aimed at children and advertising on children's television channels need to be legally restricted.

The situation regarding another important risk factor – tobacco – too remains grim. Although India has ratified the Framework Convention on Tobacco Control and has put into practice one of the toughest anti-tobacco laws in the world, the situation on the ground has not changed. All forms of tobacco advertising, including sponsorship, have been banned, yet tobacco brands are the most visible through surrogate as well as 'point of purchase' advertising. Sale of cigarettes and other tobacco products to minors goes on unchecked. So does tobacco vending near schools and other educational institutions. Smoking in public places like offices has been banned, but enforcement measures are next to nil. Stricter provisions of the anti-tobacco law have not yet been notified. A time-bound programme for the implementation of the anti-tobacco law should be developed and enforced.

Policies to Alter the Built/Physical Environment

Reports by the WHO and FAO have highlighted the importance of physical activity in the prevention of heart disease and other non-communicable diseases including some types of cancers. According to experts, 'There is clear scientific evidence that policy and environmental changes increase the physical activity levels of the entire population and prevent cardiovascular diseases.'[19] Even small increases in the daily physical activity in communities have the potential to translate into significant health gains and disease prevention at the population level.

Policymakers in the health and other sectors will have to recognize the promotion of physical activity as an important approach to tackle the rise of cardiovascular diseases. Promoting the habit of walking, use of staircases and cycling should be an integral part of the policy. This should be accompanied by necessary changes in urban design and built environment. Walking and cycling for transportation would require dedicated, safe and well-networked walking and cycling paths. These paths have to be well-lit in the evening and should have patches of shaded areas for walkers, given the extreme summer temperatures in most parts of the country. Promoting the use of public transport in place of personal ones like cars and motorcycles would also increase the level of physical activity. Introduction of low-floor, air-conditioned buses by the public transport utility has encouraged people to move towards public transport in a big way. Delhi Metro encourages its commuters to use staircases instead of elevators and escalators at its stations through motivational signs.

Educational institutions and workplaces should also promote physical activity. One could make the use of staircases instead of elevators in low-rise buildings and to move from one floor to another in high-rises. If the use of staircases has to be promoted, building owners and employers will have to ensure that the staircases are well-lit, clean and well maintained. In most high-rises with elevators, staircases are not often accessible as they are used to dump old furniture and other discarded items or used as informal smoking zones. This discourages their use. In addition, providing simple recreational facilities such as a table tennis table, a tennis court or a gym in the workplace could motivate employees to indulge in some kind of physical activity during their breaks or after office hours. Employees of central government offices in New Delhi are often seen playing card games during breaks at public places such as parks and traffic islands. If recreational facilities can be created for them in offices and if they are motivated enough, these sedentary workers might indulge in more and more physical activity.

Brazil has successfully engaged government workers in improving their physical activity levels through a programme called Agita. It began with the twin objective of increasing awareness about the importance of physical activity and increasing its levels. A campaign on radio, television and in newspapers in Sao Paulo helped create awareness. Large events and specific activities in partnership with various bodies and community groups were organized. The idea was to motivate people to undertake at least thirty minutes of physical activity every day either in one go or in intervals of ten minutes. 'The stress was on physical activity and not sport. The message was well received because we laid emphasis on moderate levels of activity. Women who used to think that sport is not for them and only for men began taking to physical activity. We got a positive response from women's groups,' said Victor Matsudo, a scientist at the Center of Studies of the Physical Fitness Research Laboratory, who led the Agita initiative.[20]

Since most people cite lack of time as an excuse for not exercising regularly, the programme encouraged people to accumulate their exercise minutes if they were not able to spare half an hour at a stretch. Media messages did not ask people to simply do physical exercise, but gave simple tips to encourage physical activity at home, while

> Providing simple recreational facilities such as a table tennis table, a tennis court or a gym in the workplace could motivate employees to indulge in some kind of physical activity during their breaks or after office hours.

using any kind of transport, in offices and during their leisure time. For instance, those who couldn't walk or cycle to work were advised to park their cars one or two blocks away or disembark from the bus one or two stops before and walk the remaining distance.

Along with motivational messages, certain systemic changes like promotion of the use of bicycles were also introduced. People were allowed to carry their bicycles in metro trains and special biking passages as well as parking space for cycles were created. The programme, whose impact is being constantly monitored, is beginning to yield health benefits. In some cities of the province like Sorocaba in Brazil, where walking and biking passages have been built and walking clubs have been started, hospitalization rates for stroke and diabetes have dropped by more than 50 per cent.

Policy Changes in the Health Sector

The state-funded health system in India continues to focus on tackling communicable diseases and services related to maternal and child health. This approach ignores the emerging disease pattern in which the share of non-communicable ailments is going up. Among the non-communicable diseases, cancer has begun to get some attention in the post-2000 period. But other chronic diseases like diabetes and heart disease have not yet been paid the same attention as malaria and dengue. Two reasons are usually cited for the neglect of chronic diseases in health policies and programmes – inadequacy of data on the burden of chronic diseases and the perception that these diseases mainly affect the rich who can afford private healthcare.[21] As a result, treatment and care facilities for heart disease were never given proper attention. This continued neglect is one of the reasons for the proliferation of such facilities in the private sector; even the poor are forced to go there.

As far as dealing with the specific risk factors of heart disease is concerned, the response of the health sector has not been very enthusiastic. Only in the case of one of the key risk factors, tobacco consumption, has there been some policy response, though the policy is yet to be implemented. The health ministry has not initiated any specific steps to discourage unhealthy diets and promote healthy food. For long, there have been national programmes sponsored by the central government to address the prevention and treatment of blindness, cancer, iodine deficiency disorders, speech and hearing problems, mental health and so on, but no such effort was made for the prevention and treatment of heart disease and other cardiovascular diseases till 2008.

Unlike all other programmes with specific targets and definite solutions, the response to heart disease prevention required multiple interventions and those that can influence people's behaviour. A national programme on the prevention of heart disease could take lessons from those dealing with population stabilization and HIV control which are also multi-sectoral and involve behavioural modifications at the individual level.

In January 2008, the health ministry launched a National Programme for Prevention and Control of Diabetes, Cardio-vascular Diseases and Stroke (NPCDS) on a pilot basis in seven districts. The Cabinet Committee on Economic Affairs, in July 2010, approved a national programme but included an existing programme on cancer control in it, making it the National Programme for Prevention and Control of Cancer, Diabetes, Cardiovascular Diseases and Stroke (NPCDCS). Various components of the programme included the promotion of a healthy lifestyle through health education and mass media efforts, opportunistic screening of persons above the age of thirty years, establishment of NCD clinics at CHC and district levels, development of trained manpower and strengthening of tertiary-level health facilities. The ministry hopes to achieve changes in the community, specifically changes in dietary patterns, enhanced physical activity and reduced intake of tobacco and alcohol.[22]

Yet another reason for the delay in translating available evidence into policies and programmes is the non-availability of standard guidelines and tools, reflecting the failure of the public health system. Guidelines are necessary to help physicians in identifying people at risk and for people to take preventive measures. Experience shows that improvements in adherence to guidelines can lead to significant reductions in the mortality rates.[23] The health ministry ought to develop appropriate guidelines for doctors and the general public about the major risk factors for lifestyle diseases – obesity, blood pressure and so on – in view of the differences observed between the Asian and white Caucasian populations. The WHO had pointed out in 2004 that, 'The proportion of Asian people with a high risk of Type 2 diabetes and cardiovascular disease is substantial at BMIs lower than the existing WHO cut-off point for overweight.'[24] The agency wanted Asian countries to develop population-specific guidelines. Yet the government did not take any initiative to formulate India-specific guidelines for BMI, obesity and physical activity as recommended by the WHO.

Resistance from private clinical establishments to public health approach to cardiovascular diseases is also responsible for the delay in developing national guidelines. In contrast, professional bodies have taken a lead in translating research into clinical practice.[25] A 'consensus statement' developed by a group of 100 medical experts from different fields is an example of private initiative. It suggested that for Indians, the normal BMI would be 18 to 22.9 kg/m2 (as against the WHO recommended number, 18.5–24.9 kg/m2), while overweight would be 23.0–24.9 kg/m2 (as against 25.0–29.9) and those with a BMI above 25 kg/m2 would be considered obese (as against the international norm of 30). New cut-offs were decided for waist circumferences too. Higher levels of physical activity – 60 minutes every day – were also recommended.[26] These guidelines were supposed to have served clinicians, researchers and policymakers dealing with obesity and related diseases till the health ministry developed India-specific guidelines.

Monitoring the risk factors and occurrence of heart disease at the national level is necessary to track the disease. This would help in developing and planning policies, programmes and strategies for its prevention and treatment. Disease and cause surveillance involves systematic collection, analysis and interpretation of data collected from the field. Such a surveillance system exists for communicable diseases and HIV but a similar fully functional system for heart disease is yet to become a reality. A good example of a surveillance system for cardiovascular diseases is the Behavioural Risk Factor Surveillance Systems established by the US Center for Disease Control in 1984. Data from this system is used to develop public health policies and programmes and to reassess them whenever needed.

> Monitoring the risk factors and occurrence of heart disease at the national level is necessary to track the disease. This would help in developing and planning policies, programmes and strategies for its prevention and treatment.

In India, a Central Bureau of Health Intelligence exists with a reasonable national network, but it is focused more on collecting health information and statistics with a view to prepare a health profile report every year. In 2007, the health ministry – with the help of the World Bank – initiated a NCD risk factor surveillance programme under the Integrated Disease Surveillance Project (IDSP) in twenty-nine states and union territories in 2007. Data is being collected on the consumption of tobacco, alcohol, fruits and vegetables, physical activity, waist circumference, body mass index, and blood pressure in men and women in the age group of fifteen to sixty-four years in both urban and rural areas.

On the research front too, cardiovascular diseases are yet to get the complete attention of policymakers and funding agencies. The country has dedicated research institutes for malaria, vector-borne diseases, tuberculosis, virology, cancer, brain, leprosy, occupational and environmental health, pathology, medical statistics, cholera and enteric diseases, reproductive health, medical entomology, stem cells, HIV vaccines and genomics. HIV has a dedicated agency – National AIDS Control Organisation (NACO) – with its own budget and implementation network, and a research centre – National AIDS Research Institute. We even have a Department of AIDS Control but there is no dedicated research institute for diabetes, hypertension and heart disease. It was only in 2009 that the health ministry floated the idea of establishing the National Institute of Non-communicable Diseases and Health Promotion Council of India.

Health education and communication is another neglected area. In 1956, India created a Central Health Education Bureau (CHEB) which has been given the job of promoting health education, communication and health-promotion efforts of the central government. Though its goal is to 'design, guide and conduct research in health behaviour', in effect it has been reduced to just being a publicity wing of the health ministry engaged in 'programmes and achievements'. The bureau is supposed to put together health education material, train people in health communication, develop educational material for schools and also conduct communication research. It has a total staff strength of sixty-one people including non-technical staff.[27]

Worksite and Community Action

A real-life experiment on how the major risk factors of heart disease play out at the individual, community and societal levels was conducted in India in ten factory sites between 2003 and 2007 by the Delhi-based Initiative for Cardiovascular Health Research in the Developing Countries.[28] It covered 10,000 people – factory workers and their family members. The idea was to modify the disease-causing factors – eating habits, physical activity, tobacco consumption – and to assess the health benefits. This

In 1956, India created a Central Health Education Bureau (CHEB). Though its goal is to 'design, guide and conduct research in health behaviour', in effect it has been reduced to just being a publicity wing.

was done with the help of interventions aimed at increasing the consumption of locally available fruits and vegetables, encouraging healthy diet, incorporating physical activity in daily lives, avoiding consumption of tobacco and its products, and maintaining appropriate body weight. Participants were also sensitized on the need to recognize and treat high blood pressure and diabetes.

First, all the participants were engaged through specially designed and developed education material, posters and banners, handouts, booklets, and real-time videos in seven Indian languages, followed by one-on-one interactions between trained health workers and employees as well as their family members. Small changes were introduced. For instance, canteen menus were modified to include salads and reduce the frequency of fried items served every week; pickles and papads were withdrawn or restricted; and on-site use of tobacco products was banned. Fruits were provided as an alternative to Indian desserts on certain days. Individuals with diabetes and other risk factors were encouraged to be compliant with treatment and were referred to a healthcare facility for further risk management.

The results were dramatic. A significant reduction in the factors posing a risk to the heart was noticed in the intervention group and not so much in the control group. There was a decline in mean body weight, waist circumference, blood pressure, serum cholesterol, and plasma glucose levels in the intervention group. The changes in related behaviour (reduction in consumption of extra salt, increase in physical activity levels and consumption of fruits and vegetables, and decrease in the use of tobacco products) could have contributed to the significant reduction in blood pressure. The results have notable implications. Translated into impact on occurrence of heart disease and stroke in the population studies, it could mean preventing about 871 'cardiovascular events' over the next ten-year period.

Besides changes in government policies in relation to risk factors of heart disease, individuals, communities and civil society groups can also play a crucial role in empowering themselves or force state agencies to take desired action. Community action can be long lasting and more acceptable than a government programme.

A number of scientific studies, in India and elsewhere, have shown that increasing physical activity reduces the risk for heart disease and diabetes. Clinical trials, under the supervision of doctors and experts, have been conducted where people with high risk were made to undergo certain lifestyle modifications and the results were noted. But can these results be applied to a community and similar benefits accrued? In order to test this, it was necessary to persuade a large number of people in a community to undergo a lifestyle modification and see if it makes a difference in their lives. Would they be able to avoid heart disease? One such community-based preventive programme was used in an experiment that began in 1996 in Chennai.

This study was an offshoot of a larger project called the Chennai Urban Population Study (CUPS), which was carried out to assess the prevalence of diabetes and its various complications among people from various socio-economic strata in the city. Two residential colonies – Tirumangalam and Thyagaraya Nagar (popularly known as T. Nagar) – representing the middle-income and lower-income groups respectively were selected for the study. Data about their health status as well as work- and job-related and leisure-time physical activity was collected with the help of a questionnaire. There were basic questions like mode of transportation to work, time spent on walking and the nature of work. The level of physical activity was then given scores in accordance with 'light', 'moderate' and 'heavy'. For instance, physical activity was tagged 'heavy' if the individual was engaged in an occupation that was

> Besides changes in government policies in relation to risk factors of heart disease, individuals, communities and civil society groups can also play a crucial role in empowering themselves or to force state agencies to take desired action.

physically demanding, walked or cycled to work or if the person exercised regularly. Those using motorized vehicles and not doing any exercise or engaging in sedentary work were classified as people who engaged in 'light' physical activity.

After the initial survey and screening for diabetes, individuals with diabetes as well as the community in general were educated about the benefits of physical activity through public lectures, video clippings, skits etc. The residents were motivated by a social worker who regularly visited the colony to exercise every day. Interactive sessions were conducted every two months, public lectures were given every three months and educational materials were distributed every six months. 'Lifestyle changes are never easy to achieve. It took both time and a consistent effort on our part to convince the members of the colony. The community realized the importance of physical activity after three years of the continuous education programme,' said V. Mohan.[29]

When the community members realized that they would have to increase the levels of physical activity they realized they didn't have a proper place for exercise. After several meetings, the colony committee decided to develop a park. They raised about Rs 15 lakh from the local municipal authorities, some philanthropists and residents. A plot of open space was identified in the vicinity and the local authorities were approached for permission to build a park there. A beautiful park was constructed in 2002 with a walkers' lane with bushes, trees, water fountains and a playground for children. Music systems were installed for additional entertainment. The residents pay a nominal amount as annual fee for the maintenance of the park.

In 2004, seven years after the initial survey, Dr Mohan did another survey and invited all individuals above the age of twenty years living in this colony to participate. Physical activity was measured once again. The results were dramatic. The proportion of those engaged in 'light' physical activity dipped across all age groups. At the baseline, only 14.2 per cent of the residents said they exercised. This number went up to 58.7 per cent, a jump of 313 per cent. The number of participants who walked three times a week increased from 13.8 per cent at baseline to 52.1 per cent during follow-up, representing an increase of 277 per cent.

Any lifestyle modification, be it smoking cessation, weight control or exercise, is the most difficult of the risk-reduction strategies to implement. The Asiad Colony in Chennai emerged as an example of how a community can be motivated to take charge of its own health. Mohan recounts the experience: 'The fact that the community itself came forward to create facilities to exercise is commendable. It has led to positive benefits by increasing physical activity levels, despite the number of persons engaged in physically challenging occupations going down. This clearly shows that the overall level of physical activity has substantially increased due to the construction of the park.' For researchers, he feels, this experience highlights the importance of sharing results of a research study with participants of the study. Treating the community as a partner can result in the community taking action and this is turn will benefit the health of its people. By altering the social environment and changing the attitudes of people, it is possible to stimulate the community to get interested in preventive health.

Like the residents of Tirumangalam colony, those living in other parts of Chennai as well as most other Indian cities and towns face a shortage of parks and recreational areas to exercise. People live in apartment blocks, and the roads just outside are narrow with no footpaths to walk on. Under such circumstances, this community-led initiative of building a park for the residents offers a viable solution. Examples like this can also have a ripple effect. When newspapers reported the success of the Asiad Colony park, communities in two other areas got motivated and built similar parks. It was soon followed by the repair of

By altering the social environment and changing the attitudes of people, it is possible to stimulate the community to get interested in preventive health.

existing parks and construction of 200 parks in Chennai city by the local administration. Smaller towns in the state then followed the Chennai model.[30]

A civil society group in Punjab has demonstrated how the physical environment of a town can be modified to make it car-free. In 2008, Fazilka in Punjab became the first city in the country to have declared its major business centre car-free. The town with a population of 70,000 has about 45,000 vehicles of which about 4000 are cars. The local body was persuaded to declare a stretch of about 800 metres in the heart of the town as car-free, following an initiative of a civil society group called Graduates' Welfare Association.

Conclusions

We need policies that are in favour of the heart at various levels – government, businesses and schools. We need policies that discourage unhealthy food and promote healthy diets, policies that don't promote physical inactivity and those that curtail tobacco consumption. Examples of what work and what do not are available. Scientific evidence exists for the government to act, though there is always a need for more evidence. Policies can be fine-tuned to suit local changes and evidence for this purpose should be generated. Population-wide changes such as tobacco control, salt reduction and curbs on trans-fatty acids can bring in handsome dividends as seen in the West. The example of Brazil in promoting physical activity can be adapted to Indian conditions. At the community level, school and workplace policies relating to making available healthy food options in canteens and providing for physical activity are also required. The example of community action in the revival of parks is worth replicating in other towns and cities that are facing a similar situation. Besides the government and the community, individuals too need to be motivated through health messages and promotion. By no means, is it a future without hope.

The Golden Age of Cardiology

In October 1982, President Giani Zail Singh went to America for heart surgery at the Texas Heart Institute in Houston. It was routine for Indian political leaders and wealthy Indians to go to the US for treatment of heart disease in the 1970s and '80s. Singh was operated upon by legendary cardiac surgeon Dr Denton A. Cooley. Between 1984 and 1991, Dr Cooley performed bypass surgeries on 625 Asian patients, predominantly Indians.

Cut to 24 January 2009. Prime Minister Dr Manmohan Singh, 76, underwent a complex fourteen-hour-long coronary artery bypass graft surgery at New Delhi's All India Institute of Medical Sciences (AIIMS). The surgery was performed by a team of doctors from AIIMS and the Asian Heart Institute, Mumbai.

The two heart surgeries are illustrative of the change that has come about in the treatment of heart disease in India in the past three decades. From being dependent on Western experts and hospitals for even routine heart surgeries, India has moved to an era where several heart surgeries are performed in medical centres across the country.

New drugs to treat hypertension and heart disease, new techniques of heart surgery, interventions such as pacemakers and medicated stents, have all made a huge difference to the treatment of heart disease over the last fifty years. Many lives are saved every day and those suffering from heart disease have a better quality of life now. The future is also promising with new stem cell therapies and possibilities of organ harvesting. Just a few decades ago, heart disease was considered a death sentence. Therefore, it is often said that we are living in the golden age of cardiology. However, new developments in medicine do not undermine the importance of prevention and the need to address risk factors such as tobacco, unhealthy food and physical inactivity and how they are causing worry. It is a better option any day to keep your heart fit and healthy rather than continue to live an unhealthy lifestyle and pop a pill every day to prevent heart disease. The argument that new drugs and surgeries are a more cost-effective option than disease prevention – advanced by some experts in the West – does not hold true in India where access to care is not equitable and affordable for everyone.

High Costs, Unethical Practices

While it is true that the heart disease burden is increasing everyday and that the available treatment facilities are inadequate, indiscriminate and aggressive marketing by hospitals is damaging the faith of the people in the medical profession. The costs of cardiac procedures – angiography, angioplasty, stenting, bypass surgery or administration of clot-busters – are prohibitively high. The high costs are to some extent due to import duties and other levies, but unethical practices are also to blame squarely.

Senior cardiologists also share this perception. 'The impression that if you go to a hospital you will end up with an angioplasty or a bypass is not entirely incorrect. Some doctors, unfortunately, indiscriminately perform bypass surgery and angioplasty. In my opinion, a lot of these situations can be avoided. But people do this for personal gains,' said veteran cardiologist Dr Bal Krishna Goyal.[1] Another senior cardiologist, Dr S. Padmavati said, 'Yes, this problem is real. They perform unnecessary angioplasties. Sometimes they do not perform an angioplasty but tell the patient they did. The poor patient doesn't even know.'[2]

New Delhi-based cardiologist Dr K.K. Aggarwal describes some unethical practices like referral fees and commission systems. 'For angioplasty with a stent, the referral fee can go up to Rs 40,000. As per the Medical Council of India Act, any referral fee, fee splitting, paying commissions or refund is unethical. But, unfortunately, most of the corporate hospitals are not governed by the MCI but fall under the Directorate of Health Services and the Nursing Home Act does not have punishment for unethical acts.'[3] He also blames a cashless medical insurance system for unnecessary angioplasties and surgeries.

In many hospitals, government employees covered under the Central Government Health Scheme (CGHS) are eligible for treatment under a few specialties. Dr Aggarwal said, 'If a hospital is empanelled only for cardiology, many of the non-cardiac patients will be admitted in the intensive coronary care unit and the diagnosis would be cardiac illness. To justify cardiac admission, unnecessary cardiac tests will be performed and the patients will be billed.'[4]

[1] Interview with author, Mumbai, 2010.
[2] Interview with author, New Delhi, 2009.
[3] Dr K.K. Aggarwal, 'Stop Commission and Increase the Fees', eMedinews, 19 April 2011.
[4] Dr K.K. Aggarwal, 'Are TPAs Making Us Corrupt', eMedinews, 18 April 2011.

The Magic Pill

The arsenal to prevent and treat cardiovascular diseases has grown considerably. The benefits of new drugs and therapeutic agents are visible in terms of a decline in heart disease and stroke rates, particularly in the developed world. But in low- and middle-income countries, heart attacks and strokes have been occurring despite the availability of new drugs due to problems associated with access and equity. People in lower socio-economic classes suffering from heart disease and stroke receive poorer treatment despite the availability of new potent drugs. In order to correct this situation, it was proposed in 2001 that new drugs that can prevent a heart attack could be more acceptable to people if they are combined into a single pill. Such a pill could contain four categories of drugs – aspirin, a beta-blocker, an ACE inhibitor and a statin – and taken once a day. This thought led to the development of a revolutionary idea called the polypill. Based on an analysis of clinical data on lipid-lowering and hypertension drugs, besides aspirin and vitamins, researchers came up with an ideal formulation of the new wonder pill – a statin (atorvastatin, daily dose 10 mg or simvastatin, daily dose 40 mg); three blood pressure lowering drugs (for example, a thiazide, a betablocker, and an ACE inhibitor) each at half a standard dose; folic acid (0.8 mg); and aspirin (75 mg). The daily consumption of such a polypill, it was estimated, could reduce heart attacks by 88 per cent and stroke by 80 per cent. Several clinical trials were conducted to test the efficacy of the polypill in different population groups and to arrive at a safe combination. In May 2011, based on a study conducted in the UK, Australia, Brazil, India, New Zealand, the Netherlands and the US, scientists reported in the journal *Public Library of Science* (PLOS) *ONE* that the combination pill could reduce the predicted risk of heart disease and stroke by half. However, researchers noted that the benefits, while huge, were not as massive as suggested in earlier studies and the side effects were also not as rare as thought at first. In the short term, about one in six people experienced side effects. Most were mild but about one in twenty people stopped the treatment after they complained of side effects, indicating that only those with a high risk of disease should pop the pill. The jury is still out on polypill.

Access and Affordability

Access to heart care, as well as its affordability, remains a major problem in India. Despite the availability of an array of wonder drugs and invasive procedures and surgeries, not every Indian in need of such treatment is actually able to avail it. A number of factors are responsible for this. A study of fifty Indian cities between 2001 and 2006 showed the shocking state of heart care in India. It was found that on an average, patients took six hours to get to a hospital after complaining of severe chest pain suggestive of myocardial infarction. In developed countries, the time taken to reach the hospital is anything between 140 to 170 minutes. Just 5.5 per cent of the people in the study used an ambulance to reach a hospital. Nearly 70 per cent of the people availed their own transport to go to the hospitals. Even if people could make arrangements for an ambulance, traffic snarls delayed them.

The ability to provide pre-hospital care is very poor. Some of the patients first went to their family physician, where they were given medication for a gastric problem. 'At the general physician level there is a "cut system" that works, which is quite rampant with private hospitals. If a patient is in one end of the city, the physician would refer him or her to a hospital in another end and not to the hospital close by,' said Dr Dennis Xavier, the author of a study published in *The Lancet*.

Once in hospital, the patient requires fifty minutes to undergo thrombolysis compared to the thirty or forty minutes it takes in developed countries to perform the same procedure. The use of key medical treatments (antiplatelet dugs, beta-blockers, ACE inhibitors and lipid-lowering drugs) is similar to that in Western countries. But there were significant differences among the poor and those with a higher economic status when it came to treatment. Fewer poor patients received treatments proven to save lives. Only a small proportion of the poor underwent angioplasty or bypass surgery.

Cost is the driving factor, be it for medication, investigation or treatment. If all patients had access to equitable healthcare facilities, reached the hospital faster, and received similar treatments, mortality rates, especially in poor patients, can be reduced.

Notes

Highway to Heartache

1. Rama Bijapurkar, *We are Like that Only: Understanding the Logic of Consumer India* (New Delhi: Penguin, 2009), 24.
2. Ibid., 34.
3. 'India's GDP Crosses $1 Trillion', *Financial Express*, 26 April 2007.
4. Dun & Bradstreet, 'India's GDP to Cross the US$5 Trillion Mark by 2020', A Dun & Bradstreet India media release, 18 August 2011.
5. PwC, 'India Entertainment and Media Outlook 2011', July 2011.
6. Rajesh Chandramouli and Pankaj Doval, 'Bike Sales Ride Past 1 mn Mark', Times News Network, *The Times of India*, 12 November 2010.
7. Asian Development Bank, 'Key Indicators for the Asia and the Pacific 2010', ADB Publication, 2010.
8. 'Mercedes Benz's Aurangabad Deal is Highest Value Car Deal in India', Autowheels.in, 14 October 2010.
9. 'Luxury in India: Charming the Snakes and Scaling the Ladders', A CII–A.T. Kearney Report, October 2010.
10. Laveesh Bhandari, 'Neither Middling Nor Muddled: A Study of the Indian Middle Classes', paper presented during the Workshop on Asia's Middle Class held at the ADB Headquarters, Manila, Philippines on 27–28 May 2010.

11. Raghav Bahl, *Superpower? The Amazing Race between China's Hare and India's Tortoise* (New Delhi: Penguin, 2010), 134.

12. '3 Billion Asians Could Become Affluent By 2050', Asia 2050 Draft Report, Asian Development Bank, 4 May 2011.

13. Bijapurkar, 232.

14. Bahl, 139.

15. 'Urban Indians "Eating Out" More: Report', *PTI*, *Mint*, 20 April 2009.

16. Bijapurkar, 104.

17. International Diabetes Federation, *IDF Diabetes Atlas* (sixth edn), Brussels, Belgium: International Diabetes Federation 2013, website: http:// www.idf.org/diabetesatlas

18. M. Ezzati et al., 'Rethinking the "Diseases of Affluence" Paradigm: Global Patterns of Nutritional Risks in Relation to Economic Development', PLOS *Medicine*, May 2005.

19. 'Key Indicators for the Asia and the Pacific 2010', ADB Publication, Asian Development Bank.

20. Nandan Nilekani, *Imagining India: Ideas for the New Century*, (New Delhi: Penguin, 2008), 385.

21. James Neel, 'Diabetes Mellitus: A "Thrifty" Genotype Rendered Detrimental by "Progress"', *American Journal of Human Genetics*, 1962, 14: 353–62.

22. 'Historical Perspective', National Commission on Population, accessed at www.populationcommission.nic.in on 10 June 2009.

23. Family Welfare Statistics in India 2009, Ministry of Health and Family Welfare, September 2009, A-21.

24. 'NCMH Background Papers – Burden of Disease in India', New Delhi, Ministry of Health & Family Welfare, September 2005.

25. V.S. Ajay and D. Prabhakaran, 'Coronary Heart Disease in Indians: Implications of the INTERHEART Study', *Indian Journal of Medical Research*, 2010, 132: 561–6.

26. 'Report on Causes of Death in India, 2001–2003', Office of the Registrar General of India, Ministry of Home Affairs, 2009.

27. Rajeev Gupta, 'Recent Trends in Coronary Heart Disease Epidemiology in India', *Indian Heart Journal*, Suppl B, 2008, B4–B18.
28. Naresh Trehan, 'Cardiovascular Disease Trend in India', a presentation, 16 November 2006.
29. Rohina Joshi et al., 'Chronic Diseases Now a Leading Cause of Death in Rural India—Mortality Data from the Andhra Pradesh Rural Health Initiative', International Journal of Epidemiology, 2006, 35: 1522–29.
30. V. Gajalakshmi and R. Peto, 'Verbal Autopsy of 80,000 Adult Deaths in Tamil Nadu, South India', *BMC Public Health*, 2004, 4: 47.
31. Interview with author, New Delhi, April 2010.
32. Abhinav Goyal and Salim Yusuf, 'The Burden of Cardiovascular Disease in the Indian Subcontinent', *Indian Journal of Medical Research*, 2006, 124: 235–44.
33. Meenakshi Sharma and Nirmal Kumar Ganguly, 'Premature Coronary Artery Disease in Indians and its Associated Risk Factors', *Vascular Health and Risk Management*, September 2005, 1(3): 217–225, published online in September 2005.
34. Interview with author, Mumbai, November 2009.
35. World Health Organization, 'Global Status Report on Non-communicable Diseases 2010', April 2011.

Understanding the Risk Factors

1. M.S. Valiathan, *Legacy of Charaka* (New Delhi: Orient Blackswan, 2003), XII.
2. Dr P. Kutumbaiah, *Ancient Indian Medicine* (Bombay: Orient Longman, 1962), 45.
3. D. Suresh Kumar and Y.S. Prabhakar, 'Heart Disease in Ayurveda III: A Historical Perspective', *Bulletin of Indian Institute of History of Medicine*, XIX: 81–110.
4. J.O. Leibowitz, *The History of Coronary Heart Disease* (University of California Press, 1970), 5.

5. Ibid., 13.
6. W.B. Kannel, W.P. Castelli and P.M. McNamara, 'The Coronary Profile: A 12-year Follow-up in the Framingham Study', *Journal of Occupational Medicine*, 1967, 9: 611–19.
7. 'Gerald M. Oppenheimer, 'Framingham Heart Study: The First 20 Years', in *Progress in Cardiovascular Diseases*, 2010, 53: 55–61.
8. Asaf Bitton and Thomas Gaziano,'The Framingham Heart Study's Impact on Global Risk Assessment', in *Progress in Cardiovascular Diseases*, 2010, 53: 68–78.
9. 'History of Framingham Heart Study', www.framinghamheartstudy.org
10. Vivian S. Rambihar, Sherryn P. Rambihar and Vanessa S. Rambihar, 'Heart Disease and South Asians 50 Years Later: A Time for Change', 2010, published online and in *Heart*.
11. C.S. Muir, 'Coronary Artery Disease in Seven Racial Groups in Singapore', *British Heart Journal*, January 1960, 45–53.
12. Rambihar.
13. Enas E.A., A. Garg, M.A. Davidson, V.M. Nair, B.A. Huet and S.Yusuf, 'Coronary Heart Disease and its Risk Factors in First-generation Immigrant Asian Indians to the United States of America', *Indian Heart Journal*, 1996, 48(4): 343–53.
14. Dr Enas A. Enas, *How to Beat the Heart Disease Epidemic Among South Asians*, Advanced Heart Lipid Clinic, USA, 2010, 86.
15. P.S. Low, C.K. Heng, N. Saha and J.S.H. Tay, 'Racial Variation of Cord Plasma Lipoprotein(a) Levels in Relation to Coronary Risk Level: A Study in Three Ethnic Groups in Singapore', *Pediatric Research*, November 1996, 40(5): 718–22.
16. Enas, 90.
17. John Shoesmith,'Who's Who: Dr Salim Yusuf', Canadian Healthcare Manager, October 2001, accessed online on 19 September 2009 at http://www.chmonline.ca
18. Salim Yusuf et al., 'Risk Factors for Early Myocardial Infarction in South Asians Compared with Individuals in Other Countries', *Journal of American Medical Association*, 2007, 297(3): 286–94.

19. Prema Ramachandran, quoted in *Nutrition Transition in India 1947–2007*, Nutrition Foundation of India, 2007, 314.

20. I. Sathyamurthy, 'Prudent Prevention and Management: Why Diabetics Should Beware of Silent Heart Attacks', *The Hindu*, 16 November 2009.

21. V. Mohan et al., 'Prevalence of Diabetes and Prediabetes (impaired fasting glucose and/or impaired glucose tolerance) in Urban and Rural India: Phase I Results of the Indian Council of Medical Research–INdiaDIABetes (ICMR–INDIAB) Study', on behalf of the ICMR–INDIAB Collaborative Study Group, *Diabetologia*, September 2011.

22. Interview with author, Chennai, September 2010.

23. V. Mohan et al., 'Epidemiology of Type 2 Diabetes: Indian Scenario', *Indian Journal of Medical Research*, March 2007, 217–30.

24. V. Mohan et al., 'Gene-environmental Interactions and the Diabetic Epidemic in India', Nutrigenomics–Opportunities in Asia, Eds E.S. Tai, P.J. Gillies, *Forum of Nutrition*, 2007, 118–26.

25. Rajeev Gupta and V.P. Gupta, 'Hypertension Epidemiology in India: Lessons from Jaipur Heart Watch', *Current Science*, 10 August 2009, 97(3): 349–55.

26. Ibid.

27. M.A. Mir and R. Newcombe, 'The Relationship of Dietary Salt and Blood Pressure in Three Farming Communities in Kashmir', *Journal of Human Hypertension*, 1988, 2: 241–46.

28. G. Radhika, R.M. Sathya, V. Sudha, A. Ganesan and V. Mohan, 'Dietary Salt Intake and Hypertension in an Urban South Indian Population – (CURES – 53)', *Journal of Association of Physicians of India*, June 2007, 405–11.

29. Enas, 115.

30. Interview with author, New Delhi, October 2010.

31. S.S. Anand, M.A. Tarnopolsky, S.Rashid, K.M. Schulze, D. Desai et al., 'Adipocyte Hypertrophy, Fatty Liver and Metabolic Risk Factors in South Asians: The Molecular Study of Health and Risk in Ethnic Groups (mol-SHARE)', PLOS *ONE*, 2011, 6(7): e22112

Of Fattening Burgers and Sweetening Colas

1. J. Boone-Heinonen, P. Gordon-Larsen, C.I. Kiefe, J.M. Shikany, C.E. Lewis and B.M. Popkin, 'Fast Food Restaurants and Food Stores: Longitudinal Associations with Diet in Young to Middleaged Adults: The CARDIA Study', *Archives of Internal Medicine*, 2011, 171(13): 1162.
2. University of California, Los Angeles, 'As Unhealthy Food Outlets Multiply, Teens Eat More Junk', *Science Daily*, 27 July 2011, accessed online on 1 September 2011.
3. 'Ancel Keys, 26 January 1904–20 November 2004', The American Physiological Society, website: www.the-aps.org
4. 'Local Food Environments Can Lead to Obesity', BioMed Central, *Science Daily*, 19 June 2009, accessed online on 1 September 2011.
5. Karen Glanz, 'Measuring Food Environments: A Historical Perspective', Emory University presentation made at the seminar on Measures of the Food and Built Environment, Bethesda, November 2007.
6. Corinna Hawkes, 'Uneven Dietary Development: Linking the Policies and Processes of Globalization with the Nutrition Transition, Obesity and Diet-related Chronic Diseases', *Globalization and Health*, 2006, 2:4.
7. Prabhu Pingali and Yasmeen Khwaja, 'Globalization of Indian Diets and the Transformation of Food Supply Systems', ESA Working Paper No. 04–05, February 2004, Food and Agriculture Organization.
8. 'Diet and Nutritional Status of Population and Prevalence of Hypertension among Adults in Rural Area', National Nutrition Monitoring Bureau, Technical Report No. 24, 2006.
9. Prema Ramachandran, *Nutrition Transition in India 1947–2007*, Nutrition Foundation of India, 2007.
10. Ibid., 134–135.
11. Ibid., 91.
12. T.N. Ninan, 'Cola Pep', *India Today*, 15 February 1985.
13. T.N. Ninan, 'Losing Fizz', *India Today*, 31 July 1985.

14. T.N. Ninan, 'Cola Wars', *India Today*, 15 March 1988.
15. Ibid.
16. BM, 'Green to Brown Revolution', *Economic and Political Weekly*, 22 October 1988, 23(43): 2205–07.
17. 'Soft and Aerated Drinks', Ministry of Food Processing Industries, website: mofpi.nic.in
18. Ibid.
19. Q&A Atul Singh.
20. Rajiv Banerjee, 'Pepsi's Rural Strategy: New Healthy Beverage with Low Price', *Economic Times*, 20 July 2011.
21. Q&A Atul Singh, Coca Cola India, *Business Standard*, 11 August 2011.
22. Annual Report of 1988–1989, MFPI.
23. Ibid.
24. Annual Report of 2004–05, MFPI, 17.
25. Annual Report of 2010–11, MFPI, 43.
26. List of grants made by the MFPI is available on its website.
27. 'Crop Diversification: A Diagnosis of the Past and Prescriptions for the Future', CII/*Technopak*, New Delhi, July 2010.
28. Uraiwan Kanungsukkasem et al., 'Fruit and Vegetable Consumption in Rural Adult Population', in *INDEPTH HDSS sites in Asia*, Global Health Action, 2009, 2: 10.3402.
29. Report of the Working Group on Food Processing Sector, MFPI, November 2006.
30. Draft Report of Working Group on Food Processing Industries for the 12th Five Year Plan, MFPI, Planning Commission, September 2011.
31. Comprehensive Industry Document on Pulse, Wheat and Rice Mills, CPCB, July 2008, 7.
32. 'Brown Rice and Cardiovascular Protection', Federation of American Societies for Experimental Biology, a press release, 26 April 2010.
33. Qi Sun, Donna Spiegelman, Rob M. van Dam, Michelle D. Holmes,

Vasanti S. Malik, Walter C. Willett and Frank B. Hu, 'White Rice, Brown Rice and Risk of Type 2 Diabetes in US Men and Women', Archives of Internal Medicine, online 14 June 2010.

34. Interview with author, Chennai, April 2010.
35. Ibid.
36. K. Srinath Reddy, 'The Effects of Globalization on Cardiovascular Disease in India', presentation made at Research Councils UK, India Office, September 2011.
37. Corinna Hawkes, 'Uneven Dietary Development: Linking the Policies and Processes of Globalization with the Nutrition Transition, Obesity and Diet-related Chronic Diseases', *Globalization and Health*, 2006, 2: 4
38. Centre for Science in the Public Interest, 'Cruel Oil: How Palm Oil Harms Health, Rainforest and Wildlife', May 2005, accessed online at www.cspinet.org
39. R. Clarke, C. Frost, R. Collins et al., 'Dietary Lipids and Blood Cholesterol: Quantitative Meta-analysis of Metabolic Ward Studies', *British Medical Journal*, 1997, 314: 112–7.
40. World Health Organization, 'Diet, Nutrition and the Prevention of Chronic Diseases', *WHO Tech. Rep. Series*, Geneva, 2003, 916(88).
41. 'NRHM is one of the Most Remarkable Achievements in Public Health Sector: Jeffrey Sachs', a PIB press release, 3 February 2009.
42. Preethi Chamikutty, 'Storm in a Bowl', *Economic Times*, 23 June 2010.
43. 'India Shopping Trends 2008: A Report by The Knowledge Company', the Market Intelligence and Publications Division of Mindscape.
44. Sravanthi Challapalli and Vinay Kamath, 'Counting on its chickens', *Hindu Business Line*, 27 August 2009.
45. 'Slump Temporary, We'll Open 100 Outlets this Year: Domino's Boss', *Economic Times*, 31 August 2012.
46. Eric Bellman, 'McDonald's to Expand in India', *The Wall Street Journal*, 30 June 2009.

47. 'Pizza Hut to Now Serve Wine and Beer Too', *PTI*, *Mail Today*, 22 August 2011.

48. 'India's Youth Savour Fast-food Chains', Amy Kazmin, *Financial Times*, 16 March 2011.

49. Pramod Kumar Sharma, 'Hazar Karod ka Ho Gaya hai Bikaneri Bhujiya ka Karobar', *Business Bhaskar*, 24 September 2009.

50. Preethi Chamikutty, 'Weight and Watch', *Economic Times*, 9 December 2009.

51. 'India Consumer Trends: Changing Food Habits 2009', *Technopak*, January 2009, Vol. 1.

52. Corinna Hawkes, 'Uneven Dietary Development: Linking the Policies and Processes of Globalization with the Nutrition Transition, Obesity and Diet-related Chronic Diseases', *Globalization and Health*, 2006, 2: 4.

53. Robert Albritton, *Let them Eat Junk*, Pluto Press, 2009, 166.

54. Interview with author, Chennai, April 2010.

55. Fact Sheet, World Health Organization, website: www.who.int, accessed 3 July 2011.

56. WHO Forum on the Marketing of Food and Non-alcoholic Beverages to Children, 'Marketing of Food and Non-alcoholic Beverages to Children', Report of a WHO Forum and Technical Meeting, Oslo, Norway, 2–5 May 2006.

57. Michael Mink, Alexandra Evans, Charity G. Moore, Kristine S. Calderon and Shannon Cosgrove, 'Nutritional Imbalance Endorsed by Televised Food Advertisements', *Journal of the American Dietetic Association*, June 2010, 110: 6.

58. *Reuters Life*, 28 June 2011.

59. Radhika Raj, 'Junk on Our Tables', *Hindustan Times*, 22 August 2010.

60. 'Nick sees 70 per cent ad growth in FY 10; eyes 40 per cent growth this year', www.indiantelevision.com, 19 May 2010, accessed on 15 August 2011.

61. 'Food and Beverage Sector TV Ads during Jan–June 2011', AdEx India Analysis, www.indiantelevision.com, accessed on 15 August 2011.

62. Tim Lang and Michael Heasman, 'Food Wars: The Global Battle for Mouths, Minds and Markets', *Earthscan*, London, 2004, 208.
63. Poojya Trivedi, 'Knorr Soupy Noodles: Testing the Fun Quotient', afaqs.com, 31 January 2011, accessed on 14 August 2011.
64. Surina Sayal, 'Top Ramen Slurps in the Crowds with "be the champion activation"', 30 May 2011, afaqs.com, accessed on 14 August 2011.
65. Rajiv Banerjee, 'Pepsi's Rural Strategy: New Healthy Beverage with Low Price', *Economic Times*, 20 July 2011.
66. 'ASCI Codes', Advertising Standards Council of India, website: ascionline.org
67. 'India: Food & Beverage Companies Pledge to Change Advertising to Children', a joint press release, 19 July 2010.
68. 'Draft Regulation on Labelling (Claims)', Food Safety and Standards Authority of India, December 2012.
69. Chitra Narayanan, 'The Truth behind Nutrition Labels', *Mint*, 22 June 2010.
70. 'Cereal Offences: A Wake-up Call on the Marketing of Unhealthy Foods to Children', *Consumers International*, 2008.
71. Documents obtained by Dr Babu V.K. from IMA and MCI under the RTI Act.
72. 'Leading National Experts Confer at Lifebuoy Symposium on Child Health', Hindustan Unilever, a press release, 4 September 2009.
73. Food Wars, 13.
74. Rajiv Banerjee, 'Pepsi's Rural Strategy: New Healthy Beverage with Low Price', *Economic Times*, 20 July 2011.
75. Annual Report 2011–11, MFPI, 5.
76. 'Food Safety: The Regulated are Regulators', *Mail Today*, 7 August 2009.
77. 'Supreme Court Ire Forces Soft Drink Executives Out of Food Panel', *Mail Today*, 9 February 2011.
78. Report of the 30th Session of the Codex Committee on Nutrition and Foods for Special Dietary Uses, Cape Town, South Africa, November 2008.

Barriers to Physical Activity

1. P.S. Shetty, 'Obesity and Physical Activity', *NFI Bulletin*, Nutrition Foundation of India, April 2007.
2. Rama Bijapurkar, *We are Like that Only: Understanding the Logic of Consumer India*, (New Delhi: Penguin, 2009), 45.
3. Tanuja Rastogi, Mario Vaz, Donna Spiegelman, K. Srinath Reddy, A.V. Bharathi, S. Meir. J. Tampfer, Walter C. Willett and Alberto Ascherio, 'Physical Activity and Risk of Coronary Heart Disease in India', *International Journal of Epidemiology*, August 2004, 33(4): 759–67.
4. D.W. Dunstan, E.L.M. Barr, G.N. Healy, J. Salmon, J.E. Shaw, B. Balkau, D.J. Magliano, A.J. Cameron, P.Z. Zimmet and N. Owen, 'Television Viewing Time and Mortality: The Australian Diabetes, Obesity and Lifestyle Study (AusDiab)', *Circulation: Journal of the American Heart Association*, January 2010, 384–91.
5. Ibid.
6. David Kohn, 'Getting to the Heart of the Matter in India', *The Lancet*, 16 August 2008, 372: 523.
7. Fred Arnold, Sulabha Parasuraman, P. Arokiasamy and Monica Kothari, 2009, *Nutrition in India*. National Family Health Survey (NFHS-3), India, 2005–06; Mumbai: International Institute for Population Sciences; Calverton, Maryland, USA: ICF Macro.
8. Rural Urban Distribution of Population, Registrar General and Census Commissioner, July 2011.
9. Yadlapalli S. Kusuma et al., 'Does Recent Migration Explain Elevated Blood Pressure? A Study among Migrants in Delhi, India', *Current Science*, 25 November 2008, 95(10).
10. S. Ebrahim, S. Kinra, L. Bowen, E. Andersen, Y. Ben-Shlomo, et al., 'The Effect of Rural-to-urban Migration on Obesity and Diabetes in India: A Cross-sectional Study', PLOS *Medicine*, April 2010, 7(4).
11. Study on Traffic and Transportation Policies and Strategies in Urban Areas in India, Wilbur Smith Associates and Ministry of Urban Development, May 2008.

12. Study on Walkability in Delhi, *Centre for Science and Environment*, 2009.
13. Auto Policy, Ministry of Heavy Industries and Public Enterprises, accessed online on 11 April 2010, website: http://dhi.nic.in/autopolicy.htm
14. Sunita Narain, 'The Nano-flyover Syndrome', *Down to Earth*, 15 February 2008.
15. Auto Policy, Ministry of Heavy Industries and Public Enterprises, accessed online on 11 April 2010, website: http://dhi.nic.in/autopolicy.htm
16. 'Study on Traffic and Transportation Policies and Strategies in Urban Areas in India', Wilbur Smith Associates and Ministry of Urban Development, May 2008.
17. NUTP 2006, accessed online at www.urbanindia.nic.in on 23 March 2010.
18. 'Pavement Stealing Road Space to be Razed', *The Times of India*, 7 May 2010.
19. 'Implementation of the Parking Policy', Environment Pollution (Prevention & Control) Authority for the National Capital Region, EPCA Report No. 25, July 2006.
20. Ibid.
21. Judgment in Rajinder Nagar Welfare Association versus MCD, High Court of Delhi, 26 April 2011.
22. 'National Youth Policy 2003', Ministry of Youth Affairs and Sports, yas.nic.in
23. 'Surge in Obesity Correlates with Increased Automobile Use', University of Illinois, Champaign, 11 May 2011.
24. James Woodcock et al., 'Public Health Benefits of Strategies to Reduce Greenhouse-gas Emissions: Urban Land Transport', *The Lancet*, 25 November 2009.

The Poison Leaf

1. Prabhat Jha, et al., 'A Nationally Representative Case-control Study of Smoking and Death in India', *New England Journal of Medicine*, February 2008; 358.
2. Ibid.
3. The references relating to historical information have been taken from 'Historical Records and Anecdotes: From the Middle Ages to the Modern Times', in Report on Tobacco Control in India (eds K.S. Reddy and P.C. Gupta), Ministry of Health and Family Welfare, Government of India, 2004, 7–18.
4. Pranay Lal, 'Bidi: A Short History', *Current Science*, 25 May 2009, 96(10): 1335–36.
5. G.K. Rath and K. Chaudhary, 'Estimation of Cost of Management of Tobacco-related Cancers', Report of the ICMR Task Force Study (1990–96), New Delhi, 1999.
6. R.M. John, et al., 'The Economics of Tobacco and Tobacco Taxation in India, Paris: International Union Against Tuberculosis and Lung Disease', 2010.
7. 'Tobacco in India: An Introductory Note, Directorate of Tobacco Development', website: http://dtd.dacnet.nic.in
8. Ibid.
9. 'Role in the Economy', Directorate of Tobacco Development, website: http://dtd.dacnet.nic.in/economy.htm
10. Vision – 2025, CTRI Perspective Plan, Central Tobacco Research Institute, Rajahmundry, accessed at www.ctri.org.in on 18 March 2010.
11. Ibid.
12. Report of the Working Group on Agricultural Marketing Infrastructure and Policy Required for Internal and External Trade for the Eleventh Five Year Plan 2007–12, Planning Commission, January 2007.
13. Report on Tobacco Control in India (eds K.S. Reddy and P.C. Gupta), Ministry of Health and Family Welfare, Government of India, 2004.

14. '"Plantation sector generates employment and export earnings", says Kamal Nath', a PIB press release, 24 October 2007.
15. 'Pictorial Warnings Can't be Repulsive', Express News Service, 17 January 2008.
16. All the letters quoted here came to light in September 2010 as a result of a RTI application filed by RTI activist Subhash Chandra Agrawal of Delhi, and shared with the author.
17. 'Azad Waging Farcical War on Tobacco', *Mail Today*, 28 October 2010.
18. Dhirendra Narain Sinha, 'Tobacco Control in Contemporary India', 29 June 2004, supported by the WHO South East Asia Regional Office.
19. M. Tiwari, 'Eschew Tobacco', *Down to Earth*, 15 May 1998, 15.
20. Dhirendra Narain Sinha, 'Tobacco Control in Contemporary India', 29 June 2004, supported by the WHO South East Asia Regional Office.
21. Quoted in judgment delivered by Mumbai High Court Bench of justices R. Lodha and D. Bhosale in Dhariwal Industries Limited and Others versus Union of India and Others on 18 September 2002.
22. Ibid.
23. 'Hookah ain't as Bad as Tea', *DNA*, 29 July 2011.
24. Cecily S. Ray, 'The Hookah – the Indian Waterpipe', *Current Science*, 25 May 2009, 96(10): 1319–23.
25. Ibid.

Call to Action

1. Theresa M. Marteau et al., 'Changing Human Behaviour to Prevent Disease: The Importance of Targeting Automatic Processes', *Science*, 21 September 2012, 337(6101): 1492–95.
2. World Health Organization, 'Preventing Chronic Diseases', 2005, 16.
3. D.A. Cohen, 'Neurophysiological Pathways to Obesity: Below Awareness and Beyond Individual Control', *Diabetes*, July 2008, 57(7): 1768–73.

4. World Health Organization, 'Preventing Chronic Diseases: A Vital Investment', 2005, 25.
5. Institute of Medicine (IOM), *Promoting Cardiovascular Health in the Developing World: A Critical Challenge to Achieve Global Health*, Washington, DC, The National Academies Press, 2010, 49–50.
6. Michael Maurice Engelgau, 'Capitalizing on the Demographic Transition: Tackling Non-communicable Diseases in South Asia', World Bank, June 2011.
7. Dr Enas A. Enas, 'How to Beat the Heart Disease Epidemic among South Asians', Advanced Heart Lipid Clinic, USA, 2010, 165.
8. K.S. Reddy et al., 'Preventing Cardiovascular Disease in India: Translating Evidence to Action', *Current Science*, 10 August 2009, 97(3): 367–73.
9. Ibid.
10. IOM, *Promoting Cardiovascular Health in the Developing World: A Critical Challenge to Achieve Global Health*, 49.
11. A. Misra et al., 'Consensus Statement for Diagnosis of Obesity, Abdominal Obesity and the Metabolic Syndrome for Asian Indians and Recommendations for Physical Activity, Medical and Surgical Management', *Journal of Association of Physicians of India*, February 2009, 57: 163–170.
12. 'FDA Proposes Draft Menu and Vending Machine Labelling Requirements, Invites Public to Comment on Proposals', a press release, 1 April 2011, FDA, website: http://www.fda.gov/
13. Reddy et al., *Current Science*.
14. The National Policy for Urban Street Vendors 2009.
15. Anuradha Kalhan, 'Impact of Malls on Small Shops and Hawkers', *Economic and Political Weekly*, 2 June 2007, 2063–66.
16. Nidhi Nath Srinivas, 'Can We Get Low-priced Pure Juice?' *Economic Times*, 10 March 2011.
17. '59% Indian Consumers Study Nutrition Labels: Nielsen', *Business Standard*, 12 August 2008.
18. 'The Truth behind Nutrition Labels', *Mint*, 21 June 2010.

19. K. Srinath Reddy et al., 'Responding to the Threat of Chronic Diseases in India', *The Lancet*, 5 October 2005, 67343–6.

20. Interview with author, Gurgaon, April 2010.

21. K. Srinath Reddy et al., 67343–6.

22. 'National Programme for Prevention and Control of Cancer, Diabetes, Cardiovascular Diseases and Stroke (NPCDCS) Approved', a PIB press release, 8 July 2010.

23. IOM, *Promoting Cardiovascular Health in the Developing World: A Critical Challenge to Achieve Global Health*, 172.

24. 'Appropriate Body-mass Index for Asian Populations and its Implications for Policy and Intervention Strategies: WHO Expert Consultation', *The Lancet*, 10 January 2004, 363(9403): 157–163.

25. Anand Krishnan et al.,'Epidemiology to Public Health Intervention for Preventing Cardiovascular Diseases: The Role of Translational Research', *Indian Journal of Medical Research*, November 2010, 132: 643–50.

26. A. Misra et al.,'Consensus Statement', 57: 163–170.

27. CHEB website accessed on 20 March 2011.

28. Dorairaj Prabhakaran, 'Impact of a Worksite Intervention Programme on Cardiovascular Risk Factors, A Demonstration Project in an Indian Industrial Population', *Journal of American College of Cardiology*, 2009, 53(18).

29. Interview with Dr V. Mohan, Chennai, April 2010.

30. V. Mohan, 'Community Empowerment: A Successful Model for Prevention of Non-communicable Diseases in India', the Chennai Urban Population Study (CUPS–170), *JAPI*, November 2006.